7 Principles To Become Your Own Superhero

7 Principles To Become Your Own Superhero

Discover the Superhero inside of you

Michelle L. Heath

iUniverse, Inc.

New York Lincoln Shanghai

7 Principles To Become Your Own Superhero
Discover the Superhero inside of you

Published by iUniverse, Inc.

For information address:
iUniverse
2021 Pine Lake Road, Suite 100
Lincoln, NE 68512
www.iuniverse.com

Creative Direction and Cover Design by Irasema Rivera
bigiranch@aol.com

Cover Photography by Noren Trotman
www.halftimehighlights.com

Makeup by Tamiko Hargrove
face2face101@hotmail.com

For Speaking engagements/book signings
contact Odette Flemming, Publicist to the author
TheOMGroup@hotmail.com
212-774-9446

Editing by Lissette Norman
LaPoetaDR@cs.com

ISBN: 0-595-15082-9

Printed in the United States of America

This book is dedicated to my grandmother Lorraine Dempsey

FOREWORD

Seven has always been my lucky number and consequently, it wasn't until I reached a whopping two hundred and seven pounds that I became fed up with my unmapped life and all its discontents. I was on the verge of committing suicide, I had high blood pressure and my marriage was clearly over. Even though the details of my life were too difficult to approach, I gave them painstaking attention and realized that there were seven things that I needed to change. I was full of fear and choked on my tears, but gradually, I gained the courage and propelled forward out of sheer frustration. Essentially, I surrendered and began right where I was. I simply began and from this was born the seven life sustaining principles that would provide a road map for where I wanted my life to go.

I was a psychological, emotional, physical, financial, spiritual, social, sexual train wreck. I was ready to self-destruct and needed desperately to change my life, but didn't know where to begin. When I mustered up the guts, I knew I would have to begin with my weight and loving myself enough to stick to a healthy diet plan. I looked like hell and could barely walk. I had aches and pain everywhere. I read self-help books and listened to motivational tapes and was inspired by Oprah Winfrey and her idea of connecting mind and body for effective weight loss. It became apparent to me that every part of me needed to be in sync in order for me to accomplish what I needed to accomplish. I thought about my life and what it stood for. I hated the way my life was going, but what could I do to change it? When careful attention was given to this question, I was overtaken with fear. I felt that changing all the negative thoughts I had been nurturing, that saving my life and loving myself unconditionally would be a Herculean task. It seemed like the work for a superhero in some comic book. Comic book superheroes were physically strong, mentally sharp and had superhuman abilities. Take Wonder Woman, for example, she was able to lasso her enemies with her magic rope and make them tell the truth, but she, like all superheroes, are not real. While it seemed silly for a grown woman to want to be a superhero, my life depended on it. I needed to create a superhero in myself that would be able to kick all the negativity out of my life and would boost my dragging self-esteem. I needed to save myself and change my life, but I was too afraid to fail.

My appetite was enormous. I was living a secret life of overeating and indulging in huge quantities of junk food. I became a closet eater and hid the way I ate from everyone. I even hid food in different places all over my kitchen. I ate an entire cheesecake and then ate a full breakfast. From a shapely one hundred and thirty pounds, I had ballooned up to two hundred and seven pounds over a short period of time. How could I live a better life? I thought. I remembered reading, "You must have silence to do this." in a self-help book. But the practice of being silent made me fearful because being silent meant going within. What if I went within and found things that scared me? A million questions danced in my mind, but no concrete answers presented themselves. Just one self-destructive thought after the other surfaced. I was exhausted and feeling greatly diminished. I hated self-help authors and their phony cheerfulness. They couldn't have been living in the real world because they seemed so unaffected by the onslaught of injustices in the world. I didn't think there was much to smile about. What was so good about morning? What was so good about life?

At 30 years of age, I had the body of a woman twice my age with a host of ailments, some I'd rather not mention. I was going down quickly. I begged my doctor not to put me on medication for my high blood pressure. I told myself I could control it by eating foods low in salt, but didn't. My doctor was fed up, but he never gave up on me. Thank God! I, on the other hand, had long given up on myself. I was lost and all that remained was a sliver of what used to be. I had lost parts of my soul in the lives of other people, in my marriage and in my job as a nurse. Everyone else's needs came first and eventually became more important than mine. I even put off simple things like using the bathroom, eating, resting, being sick, not to mention vacationing and enjoying the life that I truly deserved. Even taking my medication was hard for me to do. I needed to finish helping out a friend first, speaking on the phone and solving someone else's problems before I could do something for myself. I nurtured everyone, but me. I was last in everything. Something in me needed to suffer, to be the martyr. This was exactly why I was afraid to go within. Going within meant that I would need to silence the inner chatter that welcomed abuse. I didn't want to see how I had been participating in my own destruction. I was scared of the answers to my questions. In essence, I was petrified of the truth.

But why all the fears? I asked myself. Then I heard the old dialogue in my head, which went like this: "I'm living in America with all of its injustices, prejudices, and unfairness. I am black, female, fat, and ugly! I don't have a college degree! I'm poor as hell! My ancestors were slaves!" On and on, the negative dialogue tore me down. I believed I was not worthy of joy or happiness. The world around me reflected my pain and the chaos in my mind. I was a serious "train wreck", totally out of control and had no direction. My life seemed to be a big mess. For years, both as a single and as a married woman, I went out of my way to care for my body and to prepare for a big date or for an anniversary. It was important for me to have a clean house, to wear the best fragrance, to say just the right things and, of course, to act a certain way. I was chronically depressed and did not understand that when the home that I lived in or my mind was in chaos, every other part of me was in chaos. What came first a messy house or a messy mind? I didn't understand that every-thing is created twice. The first creation happens in our all-powerful mind and then it happens in our physical world. Most train wrecks will deny this basic truth because then they would have to take full responsibility for everything in their lives. I had an excuse for all my problems and took responsibility for none. I blamed everyone and everything else for my shortcomings and all the pain I had experienced. I believed I had done nothing to mess up my life, I was simply the innocent bystander. It wasn't until I took responsibility for what was going to happen next in my life, that things fell into place. I made choices that I felt were right and not just suggested. I stopped letting things happen and took more action in my life.

It also became apparent to me that I not only had to go within, but I also had to go back in time. I had to go to my beginnings, not just my childhood, but to the waters of the womb. I was searching for clarity, I struggled to remember what I could and was able to call up a handful of memories of when I was three and four years old. I remembered particular events, but not how I felt. I asked my mother and only got a few answers because she was resistant of revisiting the past. I needed to know about her state of mind when I was in her womb and during my early years. I could only imagine what it must have been like to be a poor twenty-six year old single mother with six kids, with an eighth grade education and living in the ghetto of Bedford Stuyvesant, Brooklyn, New York. The feelings of worthlessness and hopelessness must have consumed her. I believed my mother was embarrassed and lonely and angry. I wondered what her internal dialogue was like and all the fear she passed on when she was pregnant with me. But from what I could remember, she was a fighter. And she was brilliant. She did the best with the little she had. She prepared delicious food, we never missed a meal and we were never without proper clothing. Knowing and understanding this about my mother helped me scale the fear, anger, hopelessness and pain that I carried around with me for years. I needed to heal a lot of old wounds. It took me two long years to put the hurt in perspective. And it was then when I was ready and able to take a good look at myself in the mirror and feel love.

This book is about changing your life. It's about changing the way you think, it's about loving yourself, it's about taking care of how you look and how you feel, it's about being one with nature, recognizing your designated gifts and ultimately, about protecting yourself against all odds. I encourage you to follow the seven principles outlined in this book which serves as tools for changing your life. It will take work and requires some soul searching on your part, but a better life is absolutely possible. This book is truly for people who dare to be their own superhero and who have a strong desire to experience joy in their lives.

pErsonal equity

my strong feet carry me through the fire while
my soul's in transit so I don't
hide them in small shoes besides
they feel prettier in a poem
every day I had to say: I love my hips, I love
my thick thighs and all my sexy things until I
learned they were valuable assets
I have magical hands and
my unbridled
hair gives me a sense of freedom not yet
seen by my people
I celebrate my brilliant mystery today,
let loose my sonorous mirth while
I sit back in my chair,
turn inward and call love
my way.

CHAPTER I

THE FIRST PRINCIPLE: TO BECOME A SUPERHERO YOU MUST LEARN TO LOVE YOURSELF

Learning to love myself was a wrestling and sometimes laughable process. I began to understand the dynamic of self-negation and that when you don't love yourself; you can really do something about it. For me, it was doing everything possible to alter the way I looked because I didn't think I was beautiful enough. I had to first admit this to myself and then decided that I had to start with mirror work. I needed to take long looks at myself without attacking my nose, my hair, my lips and my skin color. This was not as simple as it sounded. I looked into my living room mirror for a few minutes and tried to imagine what it would be like to tell myself-"I love you." Again, my fears besieged me. I was all alone and thought this is silly, I do love myself! I don't have to stand in front of a stupid old mirror to prove it? But I knew that I had to. So I took a deep breath and glared at my image. In a loud, strong voice, I said, "I love you Michelle." In an instant, chills ran up my spine and I became short of breath. For years, I had expressed my love for others, but had never said those life sustaining words to myself. I looked at myself in the mirror for days. I touched and soothed every part of my weary self, every single part of my two hundred and seven pounds. I tried to look at my eyes, my nose and my lips in a more loving way because there were many times when I looked at myself and saw nothing worth caring about. I hated every part of me. I wished I had lighter eyes, smoother skin and shapelier legs. It was sad not loving myself, but with consistent mirror work, I began to embrace what I thought were imperfections.

Self-acceptance is the first and most critical step in changing your life. When you make peace with what you have, that is when you see the beauty in those things. You must accept yourself or you will not be able to move forward. You have to tell yourself that you love yourself EVERYDAY until you believe it whole-heartedly.

Loving yourself means acknowledging past decisions you've made and taking full responsibility for them, but it is equally as important for you to forgive yourself for the mistakes you've made and forgive those who have also hurt you. When you don't forgive, the burden of anger eats away at your soul and causes disease in your body. It even causes you to age rapidly and robs you of your life force and mental energy. Ultimately, it gets in the way of love—so forgive them for your own sake. Letting go of anger takes incredible courage. Forgiving not only means that you no longer blame the person who has wronged you, it also means no longer having a reason for the unhappiness in your life to continue. My friend, Tammy, for example, is embittered with her father who abused her as a child. I pointed out that if she were to forgive her father, who in his drunkenness, did not know better, she will find that it is actually her and her fears that is keeping her in an unfulfilled life. Being angry with her father gives her an excuse to stay where she is and justifies why she doesn't do something to make her life better. For her own reasons, she wants to remain angry. Loving yourself is what I call, "a life changing renaissance"; a rebirth of who you are and forgiving that allows a new you to be born.

Superheroes love themselves by getting rid of all the DRAMA in their lives. Ask yourself the toughest question: WHY ALL THE DRAMA?

If you take the time to think about it for a moment, drama in our lives is an incredible distraction from our personal and very real issues. If we stay focused on the drama, on gossip and everyone else's problems, we would purposely not have time to evaluate our own lives. We must learn to recognize when we are intentionally creating drama in our lives and then begin to stand-up and face our own issues.

Here is a great exercise that I do daily to practice loving myself. I speak to myself throughout the day as I would expect a lover or family member to speak to me with great care. (You can also do it while you're looking in the mirror). Be conscious of what you say to yourself in every instance. If you make a wrong turn when driving, or you drop and break something, do not tear yourself apart with mean words. Speak kindly to yourself. Be aware that your own words and others' words can wound deeply. Words can diminish you. In your mind, gently say, "That's okay baby girl, that was the wrong turn. Just turn around and find the correct turn." Or "Oops sweetie pie, it's just a broken glass." You can even say these words out loud. You should not have shame in talking to yourself in loving ways. Praise yourself and soothe your soul. You are worthy of praise. When your internal dialogue becomes gentler, you will feel good inside and people will begin to see your light. It will shine through even when you are not aware of it. You will not accept any less from others and people will also begin to treat you like you treat yourself.

Another way to self-love is indulging in long, hot, fragrant baths. Give yourself breathing space and relax. When you love who you are, you also love the creator in you and the universe applauds you. When you love who you are, you attract love.

You may also experience others resenting you for loving yourself. They may become envious because they don't have the courage to change their own lives. I know of marriages that have been destroyed because one partner resents the other's growth. You will out-grow other people and it may be a little scary, but don't worry. People become very critical of you all of a sudden, but that's not your issue. When I was a "train wreck" I was criticized terribly for all my chaos and when I changed my life, they still talked about me. So my point is just let it roll off your back. Deepak Chopra stated that, "You must become immune to criticism." Learn to not take things personal. Superheroes don't let what people say or think about them get in the way of their dreams. They are passionate about their destinies. They are determined to live their lives as they wish. When emotions play a part in the progression of your life, the best emotion is LOVE. When you are passionate about loving who you are, you don't focus on the obstacles. And if anyone tries to block your path to greatness, YOU RUN THEM OVER! I was passionate about losing weight and loving and honoring myself. I was so dead serious about my journey towards a new life that I even let go of some family members and friends along the road of life. I became good at eliminating from my life situations and people that caused pain or conflict. My greatest lesson was learning how to love people from afar, including family members. It's a wonderful thing. This important practice significantly reduced the stress in my life. This may happen to you, but you must decide if changing your life is worth the loss. You are vulnerable in the early stages of your process and may be easily influenced. Do not give any energy to criticism that is not constructive. The more you begin to grow in self-love, the less concerned you will be with other's opinions of you. You are not easily affected by a negative or false comment made about you because you know yourself better than anyone else. And you know the truth *you are absolutely wonderful and brilliant.* Until then, close your ears to opinions that are not passed on in a loving way.

I think I've made myself clear so far that loving yourself means accepting yourself just as you are, but I'd like to add that loving yourself also means changing the things in your life that are not healthy. Change them in a realistic time frame because the truth is there are no quick fixes in life. Women who have successfully lost weight and kept it off have had to change their entire lives, not just cutting out Thursday night burgers and exercising every now and then. I'm talking about changing everything. Every single one of us had to relearn how to eat, had to learn how to exercise properly and had to adjust to a totally different mindset. Ultimately, we all had to learn how to love and nurture ourselves. It required great effort on our part. I also want to point out that we had to be psychologically intelligent about weight loss. We had to analyze the reasons why we wanted to lose weight. Most often, weight loss is not achieved or maintained because what drives you to diet may not have enough substance to keep you focused. If, for example, you attempt to lose weight to fit into a dress for a special occasion, what will happen is, either you never achieve your desired goal or you gain the weight back after the occasion has passed. You have to find stronger reasons, and the will for a healthier life should be your main reason. Exercising and eating healthy food combats deadly illnesses such as diabetes, cancer, heart disease and other debilitating illnesses. It is a long road to successful weight loss, and it demands from you what you never knew you had. Most importantly, it can take years not days or weeks to lose weight, but the reward is an incredible sense of inner peace and personal gratification. And your soul craves this feeling all of your life, you're simply just not aware of it. But some are not ready and some will never be ready. For others, it will take a lifetime of following the false gods of advertising:

"Quick weight loss formula! 20 years of research went into this one pill. Lose 30 pounds in 1 month. It's so safe, even a child can take it." Don't believe it! Take a minute and think about it. It's harder for people to believe that you can lose 10 pounds in a healthy amount of time by loving yourself, but it's true. There are no quick fixes in life. I searched for years, exhausted most means and never found one.

Only you know if you are ready to change your life today, if you are ready to take good care of yourself and if you are ready to treat yourself special. **IT BEGINS WITH A DECISION.** You have to make a conscious decision to do the very thing that brings you joy. Loving yourself means beginning right where you are. If you are lost, overweight, confused, in poverty, in an unhappy relationship, in abuse, in a meaningless job and you are just plain old tired of how your life is going begin today! Start off by thinking about the circumstances in your life and things you would like to change about yourself. And be honest with yourself because there were times when I didn't want to change things that I knew were unhealthy for me. There are women who are afraid their lives would be worse off without their abusive boyfriends or husbands, and as insane as that sounds, it's true for many women. So get real with yourself. Next separate the things that you can change from the things you feel you have no control over. Once, you've acknowledged what isn't working in your life, what you need to let go of and what is no longer serving you, you can begin to imagine how you will address each one. You can do one at a time. There are some aspects of your life that you may not be able to change instantly, but don't be discouraged. Some things will take careful planning and that's also what loving you means.

It means being patient enough to do what is required and having faith that it can happen. You can start by visualizing what you want and seeking out information and working towards your happiness and praying for the things you feel you cannot change in your life. I'm a firm believer that when you prepare and desire something fully, you have a better chance of calling it your way. So start with you and start with love. Love yourself enough to begin right now. That is the first step in the making of a Superhero.

Just what her blues are all about

some women don't understand
the universe giving birth to.

winter & night coming early with the
silver-blue light of moon. they can't make

sense of the thousand butterfly wings
that flutter in their stomachs. changes. some
miss the beauty of it all. they don't know who
they are becoming. but me, i know.

i wait & welcome her each time.

CHAPTER 2

THE SECOND PRINCIPLE: TO BECOME A SUPERHERO YOU MUST CHANGE YOUR THOUGHT PATTERNS

There is a voice inside all of us that guides us, that warns us when potential danger is near, that builds us up and informs us of divine truths. There is a basic instinct in your gut that is wistful for your attention. Years ago, I could not hear what my voice was telling me because my mind was flooded with negative thoughts. I had some wicked self-sabotaging thoughts that governed my day-to-day experiences and clouded my outlook on life. The dialogue in my head was like a legion of enemies attacking my soul and keeping me in constant chaos. I was my worst critic and couldn't accept a compliment from anyone because I didn't believe him or her. Hopelessness, anger and fear compounded my thoughts and beliefs. I was also a worrywart and worried about everything. I was in a vicious cycle of problems because I expected the worst in every situation. I didn't understand that the mind believes what you put into it and the mind, being as powerful as it is, caused all the negative situations to manifest themselves in my life. I said things like, "My life is just full of problems, I wonder what will happen tomorrow?" And guess what, the next day another problem presented itself. Our thoughts are just that powerful. I now understand the simple mission of a thought: if you expect good, good things will happen, if you wait for the worst, trouble will find you. So be careful with your thoughts. Imagine what would happen if you took your mind off your problems momentarily and if you weren't afraid. Then you could focus all your energy on the possibility of something-wonderful happening in your life. I challenge you to try. I can tell you that one of my biggest revelations was realizing that the thoughts in my head were key in the success or failure of changing my life. If I had not done something to silence all my negative thoughts, I would have remained in the dark spaces that were killing me. I knew I had my work cut out for me–mastering my thoughts definitely required a Superhero.

I have spoken with many women who believed that they could not change their thought patterns. I was even surprised to hear medical professionals say that no one can change their thoughts. The idea that a learned behavior could not be changed is the root of the problem and if you are a negative thinker, it's easy to fall into this trap. I explained to them that changing your thoughts was possible by stopping the dialogue in your head as soon as it begins and replacing it with more loving dialogue. You cannot allow the self-defeating chatter to continue. Stop it immediately. Wearing a rubber band around my wrist and snapping the rubber band against my wrist every time a negative thought popped into my head, helped me stop my destructive inner-chatter. I couldn't believe it at first. After about fifteen minutes, I wanted to take the rubber band off because my wrist was sore. I began to grasp the idea that in the same way that the rubber band was hurting my wrist because of the negative thoughts so did the negative thoughts to my spirit. With all the years of nasty thoughts, my soul was bruised and scarred. This exercise also helped me see that 90% of my thoughts in a day were negative. How crazy! It was no wonder that my life was so screwed up. My physical world was a mere reflection of what was going on in my head and in my soul. My body language was another indication of my thoughts my posture was poor, my shoulders were hunched, and I could barely make eye contact with people. I spoke to people in a quick low monotone voice. Thoughts are just that controlling and orchestrate what occurs in your day. If you chance your day to be bad, you can really have a bad day, but if you think, "My life is good and I am blessed." or "I'll get through this and anything else that comes my way." Life becomes more bearable and, eventually, more enjoyable. It is also important to continue to repeat the positive thoughts in your head through out the day. Take, for example, a recovering alcoholic who has suddenly relapsed. What could be one of the reasons why she fell away from her recovery? The truth is this: she stopped adding fuel to the fire. She didn't keep it upfront. She stopped the positive self-talk that is required daily. She allowed the old self-destructive dialogue to creep in and breathe. She began to surround herself with the wrong people in the wrong places until they sucked her back into her old painful life. Most of us must battle our negative thoughts everyday–it is daily work. Feelings of failure and doubt will invade your thoughts, but you must push them out of your mind with the ferocity of a lion. You must be tough. For every negative thought that summons, tell yourself three positive statements to refute it. You must choose your words carefully because words have power. Your mind needs healthy dialogue in order to get you out of your predicaments. Negative thoughts are like poison and nurturing thoughts can serve as balm for your aching soul. When you stop the negative thoughts, you clear the clutter in your mind and you make room for dreams and hope and the creation of a new experience.

Another helpful practice in replacing your negative thoughts is to tape index cards with positive quotes all over your house. I had them on my refrigerator, on my dresser and bathroom mirror, on my desk calendar at work, everywhere. I had to feed myself these loving affirmations to drown out the negative thoughts. Remember that a thought precedes everything and if you want to do anything, make anything or become anything, you must first think it up and create it in your mind. You have to formulate a plan in your mind. Trust me, if you spend your truest energy on a plan, you will be and make and do whatever it is your heart desires. Some people thought we could never go to the moon. If the astronomers and the astronauts had listened to the negative mentality of others, America and the rest of the world would never have witnessed such an incredible feat.

On your journey to becoming your own superhero, you must be mindful that you are in total control of how you will respond to any situation and that your thoughts will be an important factor in that determination. Do not meet a problematic situation with a negative thought because that will only create an eruptive response. Easier said than done, right? I know. It takes practice. How about analyzing the situation fully and thinking about a solution instead. That was my problem in the past I worried about the problems that already existed in my life, I worried about the difficult situations that came up in my day and I also worried about situations before they even happened. I stayed stuck and the problems worsened because I didn't think my way out of them with possible solutions. The reality of life is that, for whatever reason, once in a while a problem may arise and your response to each problem is what you need to take a look at. If a business venture fails, if your car breaks down, if your child continues to misbehave in school, if something doesn't work out quite like you expect it to how will you handle it? I can tell you that you will not change matters by flipping your top and yelling. When things go wrong, what are you thinking? Are your thoughts hopeful? Does it cross your mind that maybe there was a lesson to be learned? Are you proud of yourself for taking a risk? Does the fact that you tried your best matter? Or do you beat yourself up for it, cry or complain? You need to be aware of what you are thinking and what you are believing when you are faced with a challenge.

If I asked you to imagine yourself doing or being something you've always dreamed of, no matter how bizarre you think it is, could you take a minute to believe it is possible? If you think it is possible, but are not sure how to achieve it, then you are on your way. The very first step is believing that anything is possible. That's where the miracle begins. I was able to make a sweeping change in my life when I began to trust my inner voice, the divine voice inside me that is essentially connected to the Creator. I relied less on the things of this world or anything outside of me. I avoided the negative thoughts of other people in my path.

I encourage you to surround yourself with as many people as possible who are supportive of your goals in life. Share your dreams only with those individuals who can offer a positive word. Do not let others place their limitations on you or cause any doubts. The best thing I did was to keep my dreams to myself when I encountered people who I was sure was going to point out all the reasons why I could fail. When an acquaintance with negative energy asked me what was going on, I said, "Oh, nothing girl!" She was not going to have an opportunity to gnaw at my ideas of becoming my own superhero. I began to believe that the wind and a beautiful sunset could be more nurturing than a human being. I thought that the universe and the Creator were moving together with me. An incredible thing began to happen when I silenced the negative chatter in my head. I experienced clarity and could understand the true power behind each thought. It took me some time to figure out, but I finally learned that with my thoughts, I could really activate my life–I could make my life what I wanted it to be. When I learned this about myself, the world around me became more luminous. I did not view life the same way anymore. I was able to enjoy small things like the sweet chirp of the cardinals outside my window and the morning dip of an insect in an open flower. Watching nature take its course brought me so much inner peace and I could not believe that I had missed out on the beauty right in my own back yard because I allowed daily challenges to overwhelm me.

I know now that my thoughts are everything and this is a basic truth for all. Superheroes know that it all begins in the mind. You must have a vision. Take time everyday to visualize what you want and how you can get it. I call this practice "vision work". When you are doing vision work for a desired outcome, begin by writing down a statement or two explaining exactly what it is you are working towards. Close your eyes for a few minutes and envision yourself being, doing or having whatever it is you desire. If your goal is to buy a house, imagine yourself walking in and out of the rooms of your dream house.

You can even put up pictures of the house you'd love to own on your refrigerator door. Gather as much information as you can about what you need to know when buying a house, or sign up for a workshop on home ownership. Make a commitment to budget and save money and, ultimately, to follow through on the required details of purchasing a home. A commitment is a promise that you make and keep no matter what occurs. Superheroes follow through with the commitments they make by staying focused on the dream, they stay focused by loving themselves enough to be patient and they remain patient by feeding their minds positive thoughts. When you keep the promises you make to yourself, you feel good about yourself and you begin to trust yourself. You also develop inner strengths. The superheroes that I talk about in this book are not extraordinary people, they are ordinary people who tap into their own inner strengths. When you begin to sort through the thoughts that fill your mind and throw out the debilitating ones, you will have the ability to recognize that your daily challenges are not just problems and life isn't just a struggle. You repair your spirit by creating a new script of dialogue and you do that by making daily deposits in your mind. When you wake up, tell yourself you are going to have a great day, even if you have to drag yourself out of bed. Talk yourself into a wonderful day. Tell yourself that you are beautiful just as you are. Throughout your day, praise yourself for any accomplishments no matter how small, tell yourself over and over that the world needs you to be just who you are. Before you go to bed, tell yourself that you will do your best to make the world a better place to live in by being the best you can be.

Promise yourself that you will coach yourself out of depression or anger or a bad mood with strong encouraging self-talk. Don't stay stuck in dark feelings and negative thoughts. You may not have had any control over what made you angry, but you can make a decision as to whether you will stay angry or you will let it go. Your attitude in life is everything. Your attitude will create your daily situations. What you think affects how you feel. Choose to bring some sunshine into your life on a cloudy day with a positive thought—that's what Superheroes do.

HAiku

Stop denying your
cup's fill & just maybe, sis,
you might be full-souled.

CHAPTER 3

THE THIRD PRINCIPLE:
TO BECOME A GREAT SUPERHERO
YOU MUST PUT YOURSELF FIRST

We, as women, are notorious for putting the needs of others before our own. For very real reasons we deprive ourselves and assume the role of "superwoman". I'd like to make a clear distinction between the superhero that I encourage you to become in this book and the "super-woman" that serves as a martyr. Women are conditioned by society to be selfless. We are taught to value the idea of taking care of the children, cooking the evening meals after getting home from a hard day's work, cleaning the house, washing the clothes and fulfilling our husband's needs with no regard for the appropriate time to care for ourselves. I battle against the image of the "superwoman" with every effort because it is a dangerous idea that only means to abate a woman's spirit. The superhero that I hope you become is a woman who is selfish, but in a healthy way. You should understand that in order for you to be able to carry the world on our shoulders, you must first replenish your soul. I challenge you to take time to do little things for yourself like eating properly, getting enough sleep at night, soaking in a warm bath in candle light and in silence, treating yourself to a pedicure or a manicure, getting your hair done or getting an aroma body massage, exercising, sitting alone at the beach or reading a book. I am not suggesting that you neglect your children or your home or your husband. Only that you make room for your dreams. How many of you dream about going back to school or taking a dance class or starting an investment club or learning to scuba dive? You need to make the things that are important to you fit into your day some how, some way. You also have to find time to be silent so that you can give your spirit a moment to rest and become clear. Don't feel guilty (guilt is a wasted emotion), you offer your children no better gift than when you are calm, patient and happy. And you can only find your peace by prescribing moments for yourself. BECOME A SUPERHERO FOR YOUR CHILDREN. Show them by example–teach them how to care for themselves and to follow their own instincts.

I've seen women who financially kill themselves trying to buy fancy cars and fine clothing while trying to fit into the big "American Dream". If only they could turn that same energy inward on themselves and see the incredible light shining in their souls. If only they could place more value on their lives and on the condition of their spirits instead of on material things that are only temporary and require too much energy to guard. When we attach ourselves to things outside of who we are, we risk the possibility of being lost when we no longer have them. When we portray a false image to elicit a desired response from others, we are floored when our true self is revealed. This is why I strongly encourage you to put your true self-first and forward. We have all heard that image is everything, but false image expends a lot of energy. We make ourselves vulnerable when we define ourselves by outside entities. Think about it—what if your house burns down tomorrow and you lose everything, what would you do? What if you lose your high-powered corporate job, who would you be? You need to define yourself by who you are and not by what you have.

Most people would fall apart if they experienced the loss of what they felt defined them. I've known of wealthy people who have committed suicide after going bankrupt because they hid behind their money and a false image. Why? They didn't even consider themselves. They put their jobs first, their cars first and ignored their true self. You have to take time to develop your spirit, to honor your purpose for being here on this earth. Your time is calculated so use it wisely. Ultimately, you are here to love, to be creative and to listen for the truths of who you want to become. Bob Dylan hit it on the head when he wrote, "He not busy being born is busy dying."

When you put yourself first, you take the time to explore and create who you want to become. For years, I wasn't sure what I wanted and that uncertainty made me fearful. Even when an idea about who I wanted to become crossed my mind, I was lacking the courage to do anything about it I didn't want to work to obtain it. It was much easier for me to lose myself in a chaotic relationship or someone else's problem. I WAS AFRAID OF CHANGE AND DIDN'T FEEL COMFORTABLE STEPPING ON UNFAMILIAR GROUND. I PURPOSEFULLY DIDN'T MAKE TIME FOR MYSELF.

Just imagine me not loving myself, housing a world of negative thoughts in my head, hating everything about my life and being scared to look at my future. I didn't want to deal with myself. People don't make time for themselves for various reasons. Have you ever heard women say, "I can't take a vacation, I'm needed here at work or at home?"

Many women do not take vacations, not necessarily because they can't afford to–there would be no financial hardship if they took off a week from work to rest and nurture themselves, but because they want to believe that they are needed and that someone's day would be wrong without them. Many people run away from themselves because they have a need to be wanted and cared for by others, but the creator has given every one of us the ability to fulfill our own needs. We should encourage others to care for themselves, we should have faith that they will do just fine without us, and we should surrender our own need to be needed.

People focus their attention on other people to take fewer looks at themselves. I went outside of myself for love and for definition. I didn't understand that these outside forces that I relied on would always fail me. That when outside forces came and went I would experience internal turmoil because they were never a true part of who I was. I also had a hard time understanding that nothing in life was guaranteed, except change. I held onto some of the most toxic relationships to avoid facing my true self, to avoid growing and changing. I didn't know that everything that I was looking for was right inside of me. Eventually, I learned that the only thing that is consistent in life is change and that change is healthy. At some point, I realized that going against the grain of life was sucking me dry. When I finally considered putting myself first, mysterious things began to happen. Closed doors opened up in all aspects of my life. In the beginning, there was resistance from the people in my life, but most of the resistance was my own. It wasn't easy letting go of my comfortable roles as the doormat, the martyr, the last one in line, the one who goes without and the one who doesn't deserve pleasure and joy. There was much to contend with. My friends thought I was self-centered. When I began to focus more on myself, others tried to make me feel guilt, but it didn't work. Others will try to keep things as they are and even attempt to interfere with your success, but push on.

Another important suggestion for considering your spirit is to celebrate all of your achievements. When you've completed a difficult task, when you begin to see changes in yourself, when you go back to school and get your degree, when you work out hard at the gym after dragging out of your house, when you finally take a risk and try something new, be sure to applaud yourself. Celebrate all the things you do. Make a big fuss over them. This will make you strong. This will create more positive energy in your life. Don't worry about losing friends, more supportive friends will cross your path. You deserve to be first. You have more to offer when you take care of yourself and continue to make yourself anew. Remind yourself that your happiness and your well being are primary. Focus your energy on creating the best person that you can be and on becoming as wonderful as you already are. Have faith that when you look closer at what's inside you, you will see that you are a miracle waiting to happen. Spend quality time with yourself and treat yourself like a queen. When you value who you are, others will take notice and will want to treat you in that same special way.

HAiku

I dreamt my beauty
eased out of me morning-like
made you feel wide-eyed

CHAPTER 4

THE FOURTH PRINCIPLE: ALL SUPERHEROES HAVE BALANCED VANITY

Vanity (van`it–`e) 1. excessive pride: conceit. That is the Webster's Dictionary definition of vanity, but I believe that vanity can be a wonderful thing as long as it's balanced. Balanced vanity means caring about your hygiene, the appearance of your clothing, your health and how you feel both emotionally and spiritually day–to–day. Balanced vanity is good for everyone and speaks volumes about a person. The American Medical Association conducted a study, which concluded that people who had a healthy dose of vanity lived healthier and longer lives. Besides, if you don't care about how you look and feel who will? You are not a baby anymore! There is no mommy or daddy to say, "Open your mouth, let me see if you brushed your teeth properly." Or "Did you wash behind your ears?" or "Have you eaten all the vegetables on your plate? There should be no one telling you to lotion your skin, to use deodorant or to make an appointment to see the dentist, etc. You don't have to wear expensive clothing to have a better appearance, you only need to have clean, comfortable and neat attire. Take pride in how you look. Mommy and daddy were our vanity patrol when we were younger and they made sure we were presentable, but now we're in charge! Some of us do well, but believe it or not, some of us do not fare so well. In this fast–paced and stressful society, the basics can be easily forgotten, but you should slow down to take care of yourself, otherwise, how can you expect others to care about you on any level? We must consider the real implications behind balanced vanity–it's another way that we express love for ourselves. With acts of self-importance, you send out a message to the universe that how you look and how you feel matters. Take on the Superhero motto: "HOW I LOOK AND HOW I FEEL ALWAYS MATTERS."

I've heard women say, "I just want someone to care about me!" And there are countless others who want to be cared for, but the reality is everyone has to learn to care for themselves. If you don't, eventually, you will become a burden on someone else. Care about yourself and do it passionately! When you behave like a true superhero and practice balanced vanity, others who care about themselves will gravitate toward you. I remember my mother saying, "Water finds its own level." In other words, you attract to your life what you are.

I met a woman who told me that she had been having difficulty sleeping for almost ten years. She also had a noticeable tic. She told me that it would cost her close to three thousand dollars to have an evaluation of her problem and that her medical insurance would not cover the evaluation expenses. She went on to say that her lack of sleep caused other problems in her life. Sleeping is the second greatest pleasure in my life (eating great food is my first) so I immediately empathized with her. Later in our conversation, she informed me that she had just won a lawsuit from a large fast food restaurant and received a settlement of almost fifteen thousand dollars. I asked her, "Why not take some of the money from the settlement and use it for the evaluation and other related expenses?" Well, she looked at me as if I had two heads. I couldn't believe it when she said that she did not want to waste her settlement money on the evaluation. She had other plans for the money and changed the subject as if it were out of the question. I continued to listen to this woman and noted that, not only did she find her health unimportant by denying herself the evaluation, but also she was grossly obese. Moreover, she was wearing clothing that barely fit and looked inappropriate. It was obvious that she did not think enough of herself to pay for her much needed medical treatment and placed more value on having money.

We have to understand that we are not made from the outside in, but from the inside out. To achieve balanced vanity, inside work is also required. It is not only your hair and the way you dress, it is much more than that. Balanced vanity is a way of life. It means being healthy in every way. It means going to the dentist for routine check ups, and not every five years, but you have to visit the dentist every year at least one time. You should have a yearly physical, you should see a dermatologist if you have an unexplained skin disorder. You should have your annual physical and gynecology exam. And of course if you are due for your mammography schedule it and get it done! There are men and women who look in every mirror that they pass. They spend hours grooming themselves. Their entire focus is on what others think of their appearance, but what's really going on inside? Balanced vanity means mending what's inside and cleansing your spirit.

Your soul needs careful attention, even more so than your body. Some may find it embarrassing to admit, but I have no problem saying that I went to therapy. I believe it was one of the best things I ever did for myself. Initially, I hesitated going to counseling because I thought it was only for crazy people and I plopped all my issues on my husband's lap for analysis, but I realized that he couldn't be everything to me nor was he trained to help me. I needed a professional to sort through, organize, clear up smooth out and help me resolve all my issues. I needed to look at all the uglies in my closet. I needed desperately to make peace with matters that haunted me.

My spirit is healthier today. I know that going to a psychologist can be expensive and seems only for the privileged, but there are therapists that are willing to work with your budget, you just have to call around. Choosing to go to therapy is another act of balanced vanity and is just as important as going to see a dentist for a toothache.

On the other end of the spectrum, you also find the self–consumed individuals who are not too concerned with others. Their lives are significantly turned inward, they see some things only in terms of how it affects them. Most of their sentences begin with "I" and their conversations are one-dimensional. I remember calling a friend to tell her that my gynecologist had done a procedure on me to rule out cancer. I was nervous about the results and, at the moment, just needed an ear. She brushed off my anxiety by saying, "Stop having negative thoughts!" And while I felt I taught her well, I didn't appreciate the fact that she immediately created an opportunity for us to focus on her. This wasn't unusual. When she said, "You won't believe what happened to ME when…" I slammed the phone down. She eventually became one of those friends that I learned to love from afar. It was always about her and she was too full of herself to feel for anyone else. Those of you who tip the vanity scale need to be more aware and sensitive to others at all times. Become better listeners and learn to be more humble.

Women who do not respect themselves, who allow others to abuse them whether, verbally or physically and women who abuse drugs are not demonstrating balanced vanity. These forms of abuse make it clear that they do not see the importance of caring for their bodies, their health and their spirits. Other forms of abuse include allowing someone to speak to you in a disrespectful manner, allowing others to control what you say and do, and accepting infidelity. These are clear forms of abuse, yet many women overlook them because they don't want to make waves and don't have the courage to assert themselves. These women lack self-esteem and while they don't like the abuse, they don't care enough about themselves and lack the necessary tools to do what needs to be done for themselves, even if it means making big, rough waves.

There is no reason why anyone should stay in an abusive situation. If you are in an abusive relationship, ask for help from others, begin to take steps away from your abuser or take long leaps if you have to, but do something. Begin to lessen the time you spend with anyone who is not loving towards you. Then focus on yourself until you can see that you are worth more. Find the value in your spirit. Begin right where you are. Take care of all matters that have to do with you. Think like a Superhero—rely on yourself and have faith in God. We all have the capacity to direct and improve our lives, we have to look closely at our behaviors, habits and practices and measure each against the idea of balanced vanity. I've heard it said that, "Faith can move mountains" and, while I've never actually seen mountains move, I have been witness to the kind of faith that changed my life.

mothers sow lilac
and pray for their daughter's full
bloom before they die

CHAPTER 5

THE FIFTH PRINCIPLE: ALL SUPERHEROES CARE ABOUT NATURE. THEY KEEP OUR WORLD HEALTHY AND ALIVE.

I discovered a marvelous source of energy almost by accident. Whenever I became angry, my immediate response was to get away from the situation that angered me and usually, I went for a long walk. I'd huff and puff through the park cursing and replaying the argument in my mind over and over. I would go on in my head thinking, I should have said this and that. Meanwhile, the earth waited patiently to be seen. After about half an hour, I could feel the universe working me into a peaceful calm. I easily slowed down my pace to the incantations that resonated in the wind.

Soon after, my anger had been surrendered and released and I could finally notice the flowers, the butterflies, the tall maple trees, the fast-moving squirrels and all the beauty under the sky's spread. Now I go for walks on the beach or in the park for serenity, to clear my thoughts and to gain strength.

Humans benefit tremendously from the simple miracles of nature. The trees and plants in our world help us breathe. Every insect, bird and plant plays an important part in balancing our ecology. The ocean also offers healing powers. If you sit by water when you are hurting, you'll find that the water lends its soothing energy and washes away your pain. Mountains, deserts and rain forest are our ecological parents. Even devastating tornadoes and hurricanes have their reason. God created more than a million other wonders in the world and we must find the time to reflect on them. Just the mere observation of nature can recharge your spirit. Have you ever seen an orange-red sunset gently eat time? Have you ever heard a bird's song? By paying closer attention to the universe, I could see it becoming more aware of me. In the morning, I sprinkled breadcrumbs in my walkway for the birds that gathered in a nearby tree and I believe they sang songs for me. We are so connected to nature. Just as a flower needs water and sunshine to grow, so do we.

Beaches, wooded parks and mountain ridges have their own rhythm. I tune in whenever I go for long walks with my dog, Souli. Nature has its divine way of silencing my thoughts. Now, I can say that I depend on nature's offerings. No matter what the weather is like, you can find me walking close to the beach's surf, looking for my peace in the consistency of the waters. People think I'm crazy because even when it's snowing, I'm out early in the morning drawing from the ocean's tide, but communing with nature really fills my spirit. I can see the difference in my attitude at work on the days when I've had my morning walk and on the days when I haven't.

We must learn how to live in harmony with our environment. The health of our natural environment is so significant and it troubles me when I hear people say, "I'm not going to clean up or recycle because I can't make much of a difference." There was a time when I believed I couldn't make a difference in saving my environment either. That is until I became tired of all the litter thrown in my street. There were candy wrappers, empty bottles, cigarette butts, fast food containers and a lot of other waste and I refused to look at it everyday. I wondered what I could do in my own neighborhood, how I could make it better. I decided that I would clean up the garbage in front of my house. Then eventually, I cleaned the front of the next house and the next one over until the entire street was spotless. That was only the beginning. Soon, others on my street took part and, finally, our street became the cleanest in the neighborhood. It was great that I had influenced others by taking the first step. We all have the power to make a difference. Make a conscious effort to recycle. We should participate in keeping our home, our streets, our neighborhoods and our world clean.

If you have flowering gardens smell the flowers and witness their beauty. If you don't, find some time to visit your local botanical garden or start a community garden.

Take care of and nurture your garden, pull the weeds out and till the soil. Plant your favorite seeds, and watch them grow. You can tend to a host of window plants or you can treat yourself to flowers. I have a ritual whereby every payday I buy myself flowers. I'm fascinated by the casual grace of callalilies, the smells of hyacinths are heavenly and tulips add beauty to any room. Plants and flowers give your home brilliant energy and gladden your spirits. You will marvel at the splendor of this form of life. Learn to appreciate and be one with nature. Find time to sit in a park or in front of a lake or in your own back yard and meditate. In the silence, you can seek the answers to most of your questions or you can just rest your thoughts on nature's ground.

Focus on your breath and work to quiet the mind. Be still and believe that the glorious elements of nature will assist you. If we take care of our natural environment, it will take care of us. The poet M. Connellan said, "I am the trees from which I bud next May." Know that you can make a difference in preserving the beauty in our world for generations to come. We are all equally responsible for making contributions to the environment. The beauty or ugliness around you is a reflection of what's in your soul, so make the choice to let the most beautiful shine through. Become the Superhero who makes a difference in protecting our world.

utterances

Either I walk my journey or I'll be dragged along-this
is a truth that would not be lost again. I did not want to
be a writer and usually found myself a broken seeker.
the belated rain of winter lore reminded me that I had

wandered from His will. Not writing became like living
later and there was no language for wounds or a kiss
or a memory tumbling forth. I fell far from my source
and life passed as though it were simple, but with so

much road to travel still, I know I must write. I have to
because I will die otherwise. I pray that my guts catch
up to my mission in life and hold onto the whisper just
beyond the page: My life-work is who I am

I surrender to my purpose and write what moves in my
soul. The rest, I leave in Gods hands.

Chapter 6

The Sixth Principle: Every Superhero Understands that They have been Given Gifts And They Utilize Them

Our creator has endowed every one of us with unique gifts and talents. We are each here on this earth to do something in our own special way. Whether we are painters, writers, chefs, negotiators, party planners, healers, or those of us who can retain a wealth of information, we are all given gifts with the intent that we will use our gifts to help and heal others. The bible states that "We are all vessels through which God pours his sweetest wine." I have come to believe that it is the desire of our Higher Power that we allow ourselves to be used to serve with our gifts. Although many of us have gotten in our own way or have ignored our talents, it is never too late to tap into your spirit to find your hidden gifts. Our gift is our mission in life and our

mission is who we are. It took me a long time to understand this concept. In many of my lectures, I've spoken to
artists who treat their divine gifts as a hobby because they
don't have faith in them.

They don't utilize their blessings and their lives are
stressed from working in meaningless jobs that pay the
bills. I tell them to find the courage to hone their talents
and have more faith in their gifts. Do what you love and
you will be rewarded. But how does one find their gift?
Well, I went to nature to listen for mine. I began to discover my own gifts during my walks near the water's edge
at the beach. The honest truth is that a writer's task, for
example, is to sit silently and wait for the words to pass
through them and then write them down. It sounds simple, right? It can be, but a faithless writer will experience
writer's block because she doesn't believe that she can
touch lives with her gift and live off of her talents. I love to
quote Mike Phillips in this case: "Money will come when
you are doing the right thing." We are all here to create. If
you are a writer or a musician, it is through this medium
that you will find higher truths. Do what you truly desire
to do. There is where your riches lie. Follow your gut. Our
true self is waiting inside to be discovered, to be heard, to
be gently spoken to and to be given a break from the day-
to-day pressures of life. Every Superhero makes it their
business to seek out her special gifts. That's what makes us
"Super." Other ways to discover your gifts are through trial
and error. Do the things you love, take a class, and try different things that interest you. Pay attention to the activities that feed your spirit. I made a promise to myself that
my next career will be the kind of work that I look forward
to and don't want to stop doing at the end of the day.

Why are gifts and talents so essential? Why do we have to discover and utilize them? Initially, I didn't think it was important, until I discovered my own. Our gifts open us up to receive blessings for ourselves and for others. When we are creating what we love and focusing our attention, we are open channels. Our Higher Power takes advantage of this opportunity and spills miracles through us. If you are working at a job that is not fulfilling, for the sake of paying your bills, you should consider what you'd rather be doing if you were not afraid to simply quit, and then begin to explore the idea further. You can begin by just thinking about your dreams and your innate powers.

Women are God's beautiful gift to mankind. We have been blessed with the ability to house, nurture and birth nations. Every person you see has come out of a woman's body. This is the first divine gift of all women; we are creators by nature. Women are also intuitive and mystical. We are gifted beyond measure. If someone refers to you as a witch, take it as a compliment. The mystical powers of witches were not understood and, subsequently, feared and that fear led to the burning of witches many years ago. Even some religions today regard women as less valuable than men. I believe that man created this idea to give men superiority and dominion over us. But we are finally wising up. Women trust their intuition and are creating more and believing in themselves more today. We are finally realizing that if we can produce the miracle of life, we have the power to become whatever we want and to change the world. In "Mothers, Leadership and Success", Guy R. Odom goes on to say, "Research on each individual living today, who has achieved high success and whose leadership and dominance is thereby recognizable, would show that in varying degrees his or her mother is the root of such achievement." Yes, every women, every mother, wife, sister and daughter is a gift to the world. We are incredible! We are the creator's prize possessions. We are all the essence of LOVE. We hold the miracle of life in our bodies. We are Superheroes by nature and I encourage you all to claim it. Talk like a Superhero. Demand respect like a Superhero. Be fearless like a Superhero. Begin to demand more of yourself. Teach your children, both girls and boys alike, about the truth and value of women. If you can create a human being, image what else you could create.

Celebrate your womanhood and the gifts that come with it. I smile and laugh at the idea that God makes no mistakes. I was made as a woman for many incredible reasons and so were you. I was created so that I too can create and love and heal others. You are God's glory. You are the world's hope. Your gifts and talents are the possibility for peace and joy in this world. God has granted all of us with gifts and it is our duty to utilize them in our appreciation of them.

warning

It rises from the hard times that
Hide too long in a woman's smile.
How bloodshed occurs is not strange.
Nor does it happen

By accident. Sleeping with one eye
Open, mining her soul for palpable
Images of survival, she will consider your
Death each time you mistake

Her for prey. She is vigil of the one's who
Intend to slow her down until she
Loses her meaning and who, even sooner, intend
To kill her faith until she loses her

Laughter. How bloodshed occurs is not
Strange at all. Nor does it happen by accident
And if it surges from a woman's compromised
Splendor, nothing can save you.

CHAPTER 7

THE SEVENTH PRINCIPLE: ALL SUPERHEROES ARE ACUTELY AWARE OF THE IMPORTANCE OF PROTECTING THEMSELVES

This final principle offers significant ways to shield yourself from the day-to-day pressures of life and to safeguard any changes you have made. The idea behind this last principle is to provide additional practices that will compliment all the other principles in this book. I provide ten ways in which you can protect yourself from straying from your life-changing mission.

1. Television: Minimize and monitor what you watch on television. Focus on quality programming. I have eliminated harmful and false programming, from my psyche by minimizing the time I spend watching television. Women are fed false images of who we are. We are frequently portrayed as vulnerable, weak and needy. We are constantly depicted as sex objects and women are too often shown murdered and brutalized in television movies. Television idealizes death and violence and is now practicing loose judgment when it comes to sex. I believe that watching excessive amounts of television that is not positive or life enriching programming, is dangerous overall and creates undue stress in our lives.

2. Phone: The phone is another big distraction. For me, unnecessary phone conversations came to a halt when I started changing my life. I began to understand the importance of simply not speaking. I learned to enjoy silence that quieted my exhausted soul. I also enjoyed watching my phone bill go from an all time high of $350 dollars a month, to a crashing low of $40 dollars a month. I no longer use the telephone to keep myself occupied. I focus on my goals, instead of trying to solve someone else's personal problems on the telephone! I keep my phone conversations to a minimum and spend more time on what needs to be done in my own life.

3. Procrastination: There's no other way around it, you simply must do what you don't want to do and get it out of the way! When I put off what I have to do, the tension builds because in the back of my mind, I'm worrying about it. I lose energy when I procrastinate. Develop a daily or weekly "Things to do" list and stick to it. Break up your goals and take it one step at a time. You will find that after each step, you will feel better. Stop putting things off. If you continue to put things off, you need to explore why. When you follow through with all the things on your list–REWARD YOURSELF!

4. People and Things: Stay away from people who zap your energy. You know who the needy people are and who relies on you emotionally. This will not be easy especially with people that you love, but as I told you–love them from afar. Susan Taylor, Editor-in-Chief of Essence magazine, gave me this advice four years ago when I called her. Even the things in our lives that are not functional and are only taking up space in our homes need to be given away or sold to someone who can use it. Make room in your life for new things. Keep only what is meaningful.

Get rid of the things that you don't use. You live on this earth for only a period of time, make it wonderful and as light a load as you can.

5. Preparedness: Try to be ready for all that comes your way. Be proactive. Prepare your clothing and meals for the upcoming week. Prepare your bills to be mailed. Research a company before an interview. I prepare my mind, my soul and my body for my daily challenges. If I know I have a speaking engagement coming up, I get ready for it. I don't wait for the morning of the event to think about what I'm going to wear. I prepare the night before. If I have more involved goals, I pray and gather all the necessary information and get myself as ready as I can to tackle whatever I set out to do. Prepare yourself so that when an opportunity presents itself, a miracle can happen.

6. Organization: You must keep your life organized. The time you spend searching for something is time wasted. My friend, David Williams, once said, "Being organized is the ability to find anything in your file cabinet or your home in thirty seconds sharp." I'm still working on that, but in order for your life to be organized, everything in your life has to be in order. The order of your closet and drawers in your house are a mere reflection of your inner self. I strongly encourage you to organize all the drawers, closets and cabinets in your house, car and workspace as a representation of your organized internal state.

7. Relationships: The best relationship you can have is the one with yourself. Be loving, forgiving, enjoyable, peaceful and giving with yourself. Your relationship with your body is also of optimum importance. It is the vehicle, which carries your mind, soul and spirit. Before you can have a productive relationship with another person, you must love yourself. You have to know yourself and be fully aware of what you bring to the table. When you are not clear with yourself and you are not sure why you enter into a relationship, you will only create great confusion in your life and in the life of your partner. It is also very important to have a good relationship with a higher force than you, no matter what your beliefs are. Relationships may not always be peaceful, but you should both work toward peaceful times, they should not rob you of energy and drain you. If there are problems in your relationship, you can seek therapy or other methods of resolution, but if your partner is not trying to resolve a continuous problem, consider the future of your relationship. You can usually tell if a person is right for you on the first date. If you know that it's not going to work, don't go on that second date. Don't do it. If you have an idea on your first date that they are trouble, that they are abusive and will suck you dry–run away from them fast! Before you begin a relationship, also be clear with yourself and your past partner that the relationship is truly over. Give yourself some time in between relationships to heal and to regroup. Don't lose yourself in a relationship either. Remember and stick to your plans no matter what.

8. Respect Money: You must learn to save and not spend all of your money. Save for a rainy day. If an emergency presents itself and you do not have money, the emergency only becomes more stressful. As women, we should always have emergency funds. This will ensure our independence. Saving a set portion of your weekly or monthly income should be the first bill you pay. It should be a regular bill that you pay yourself. Even if you are married and depending on your husband's income, you should continue to build your savings. Always be as prepared as you can be financially. If you decide to save $20 dollars a week, in one year you will have saved $1,040 dollars. In five years, you will have $5,200. If you can save more, do it. If you can only save $5, it doesn't matter, save something. When you have money saved, you feel better, you feel safe. Learn to depend on yourself. Empower yourself and you won't feel vulnerable to the vagaries of life changes. It will not be easy, but seek financial changes in your life. Learn how to handle your finances and stop waiting on the Lotto for your riches. Try to pay your bills each month and pay them on time. The spiritual law of abundance stresses that you must pay for everything you receive and by paying for what you receive, you show your appreciation. Don't try to cheat anyone or steal because there is a Higher Power that watches everything and can withhold your abundance from you. You deserve financial abundance and wealth begins in your mind. Even when you don't have money in your possession to pay a bill, believe in abundance and work toward it. Don't underestimate the power of God. You can suddenly find a check in your mailbox from someone you helped out years ago. I have faith that I will manage financially and my Higher Power always comes through. One day at work a coworker asked me "Michelle, how do you manage? You only work two days a week." And without hesitation, I answered, "I have abundance." She looked at me rather strangely. I knew this was not the answer she was looking for, but that is what I truly felt. We all have abundance. Try to find ways to achieve your financial goal. Gather information and learn more about investing your money. Seek professional help and watch carefully as your money grows. Start now. Save your money and keep it like a Superhero keeps her strength and gifts.

9. Prayer and Meditation: Pray and meditate. Have your own private conversation with God. Stay in constant dialogue. Begin each day with a prayer before you get out of bed. Know that you are not in this alone. When I follow the divine voice inside of me, I do well in life's daily challenges. Pray and be thankful for all the blessings in your life. Be thankful for each meal, for your safe arrival, for the luxuries in your life, for your family and friends, for the peace in your home, for who you are and who you are becoming. Before you go to bed be thankful that you made it through another day. Be thankful for the little things. God gives you more in life when you show your appreciation and you can do that in prayer. Meditate and clear your mind as often as you can. Find time to quiet your mind and let God in to speak to you and provide some of the answers to your questions. Sit still to replenish and refresh your soul.

10. Caring For The Physical Self: Exercising is so essential to the body, mind and spirit. Even as little as twenty minutes a day is great. Do something, anything. Try Yoga. The feeling that you will get from challenging yourself physically is indescribable. It builds self-esteem. It produces chemicals in your body that make you feel good. You must become passionate about your health and well-being. Begin your mission to become your own Superhero today. Refrain from dragging someone into your workout schedule unless you will be working with someone who is more motivated than you are. Working out with others is fine, but always agree to meet at the gym. Read books on working out or weight lifting, these are your best partners. If you exercise daily and feel better as a result of it you will find that you interact with people in a different more loving way. I became a superhero by training at the gym. In the aerobic classes that I taught, I stressed to everyone that **NOTHING SHOULD GET IN THE WAY OF YOUR EXERCISE TIME.** If you have to visit someone who is sick in the hospital, go to the gym first, work out and then visit the person in the hospital. If your job is stressful, go to the gym and work out. In this way, you can prevent the little nervous breakdowns.

When you are on a mission, it is of utmost importance to keep your plans to yourself. Write it in a diary. A food diary is a big help. You can begin to become aware of your eating patterns and eventually can figure out what is actually eating you. Also, prepare your foods lovingly and with care. Eat a lot of variety to keep your meals interesting. I'm big on variety and I eat a lot, but I only eat twice a day. I eat a good breakfast and a huge vitamin and mineral packed lunch. This is the way I maintain my weight. It works for me, but it may not work for you. Find a diet that works for you and stick to it. Exercising and eating right is so important in protecting yourself. You must also drink plenty of water and get lots of rest. I researched ways in which to get plenty of rest and sleep. There are experts at the Mayo Clinic who have a wealth of experience with this subject. This world-renowned hospital is made up of some of the top experts in the field. This way of protecting yourself is the last and most important of the Seven Principles and it is the one principle in particular that I am asked most often about. Everything may not work for you, but some things may. First, I will help you to understand the factors of weight control.

Were you born to be fat?

When you eat more calories than you use through activity, you gain weight. But as simple as it sounds, you can't assume that everyone who's overweight eats a lot.

Being overweight stems from the interaction of several factors:

- **Genetics**—Genes play a part in how your body balances calories and energy. Children whose parents are obese tend to be overweight too. A family history of obesity increases your chances of becoming obese by about 25 percent to 30 percent.

Heredity doesn't destine you to be fat. But by influencing the amount of body fat and fat distribution, genes can make you more susceptible to gaining weight.
Researchers are examining the role genetic mutations may play in causing some obesity. Genetic defects have been found to affect levels of leptin, a protein that helps regulate metabolism and appetite. However, it's not clear yet if altering leptin levels would help in treating obesity.

- **Gender**—Muscle uses more energy than fat does. Because men have more muscle, they burn between 10 percent and 20 percent more calories than women during rest.

- **Age**—As you get older, the amount of muscle in your body tends to decrease, and fat accounts for a greater percentage of your weight. This lower muscle mass leads to a decrease in metabolism. Your metabolism also slows naturally with age. Together, these changes reduce your calorie needs.

- **Cigarette smoking**—Men and women who smoke tend to weigh 6 to 10 pounds less than nonsmokers. After quitting, weight generally increases back to the level of nonsmokers. Weight gain after stopping smoking may be partly due to nicotine's ability to raise metabolic rate. When smokers stop, they burn fewer calories. Another reason former smokers often gain weight is that they generally eat more after they quit. However, the advantages to your heart and lungs from stopping smoking far outweigh the risk associated with moderate weight gain.

- **Physical inactivity**—Overweight people are usually less physically active than normal-weight adults. Inactivity isn't always the cause of obesity, but lack of exercise can be the result of being overweight.

- **High-fat diet**—Ounce for ounce, fat provides more than twice as many calories as protein or carbohydrate (9 calories vs. 4). This energy difference may explain how fat promotes weight gain. Yet, even when caloric intake is the same, a person eating a high-fat diet tends to store more excess calories as body fat than someone eating a lower-fat diet.

- **Medical problems**—Less than 2 percent of all cases of obesity can be traced to a metabolic disorder such as low thyroid function or hormonal imbalances.

Overweight versus 'overfat' Traditionally, "overweight" has been defined as weighing more than the "healthy" weight listed for your age and height in a weight table, but that doesn't account for differences in body composition.

For example, athletes are often "overweight" by weight table standards because of a large frame or muscle development. But they aren't overfat.

We've learned that body fat, instead of weight, is a better predictor of health.

Although chances are if you're overweight, you're also overfat. Simply stepping on the scale won't tell you how much of your weight is fat or where you're carrying that fat. And those are both more important factors in determining health risks than weight alone.

In healthy adults, acceptable levels of body fat range from 18 percent to 23 percent in men and 25 percent to 30 percent in women.

But weighing yourself tells you little about how close you are to that mark. Gaining or losing a pound doesn't always mean a pound of fat. Small, frequent shifts on the scale typically reflect fluid changes.

Your body fluid levels vary depending on the amount of salt you eat, your activity level or even changes in the weather. You can also lose fluids after drinking certain liquids, such as coffee, that act as diuretics.

Emphasis on the health risks of excess fat vs. excess weight has led to the popularity of body fat testing. The key to body fat analysis is having fat estimated by a trained professional using a reliable method, such as skinfold measurements, infrared interactance, bioelectrical impedance or underwater weighing. Yet all methods only give you a ballpark figure. The older you are or the more fat you're carrying, the less reliable the measurement may be.

A combination of three assessments you can do at home—the body mass index (BMI), a waist circumference and a personal and family history—can give you a good idea of whether you might enjoy health benefits from losing weight.

Health effects of obesity

Each of the 30 or 40 billion fat cells that make up your body is a collapsible thin-walled tank. Most of the extra calories you eat that you don't need for immediate energy are stored as fat.

If you hunted and gathered your food, excess fat could come in handy when food was scarce. You could simply tap the energy stored in your fat cells.

Yet, that's hardly the case today. Food is available year-round. And few Americans wait more than several hours between meals or snacks. Your unlimited capacity to store fat can have a profound effect on your body. The more your weight increases, the more problems you'll face in staying healthy and living longer.

Shortness of breath may be the first sign of strain placed on your body by excess fat.

As fat accumulates, it crowds the space occupied by your organs. Some obese people cannot sit comfortably because of fat accumulation in their abdomen. In a sitting position, the lungs have limited space to expand while breathing.

Obese people—even moderately overweight men and women—constantly put an extra burden on their backs and legs. Eventually, this can aggravate degenerative arthritis (osteoarthritis). Complications following surgery occur more often in overweight people vs. those who aren't. Wounds don't heal as well or as fast. And infection is more common.

Obesity increases your resistance to insulin and is a leading cause of noninsulin-dependent diabetes. Your liver makes more triglycerides and cholesterol if you're overweight. In turn, your risk of developing gallstones increases. Excess weight makes you more vulnerable to high blood pressure, cardiovascular diseases such as coronary artery disease, stroke, and early death.

In a country that relates beauty, intelligence and success with thinness, being overweight also has emotional and social consequences. It's not uncommon for over-weight adults to experience psychological stress, reduced income and discrimination.

Preventing Heart Disease

Obesity is a 'major risk factor' for heart disease. Obesity has serious implications for you health. It has been linked to increased risk of diabetes, cancers of the prostate, colon and uterus, complications follow-ing surgery and to aggravation of symptoms of osteoarthritis. Obesity is also a major risk factor for cardiovascular disease.

"Obesity is as dangerous for the heart as smoking, high blood pressure, high cholesterol and a sedentary lifestyle," says Brooks Edwards, M.D., a cardiologist at Mayo Clinic, Rochester Minn., and medical director of Mayo Clinic.com. He adds, "As a society, we are digging our own graves with our forks and spoons. We're eating more and exercising less."

Despite exercise videos, diet pills and low-fat foods, Americans are fatter than ever. A study published in the May 29, 1998 issue of the journal Science found that 54 percent of all U.S. adults are overweight—an increase of about 33 percent since 1978.

The study also found that more than 25 percent of the nation's children are overweight or obese, accord-ing to James Hill, a nutritionist at the University of Colorado Health Science Center in Denver and the study's lead author.

The definition of obesity—being seriously over-weight—varies among researchers. Calculating your body mass index (BMI) can help you determine whether you're overweight.

"Obesity itself has become a lifelong disease, not a cosmetic issue, not a moral judgment—and it is becoming a dangerous epidemic," says Robert H. Eckel, M.D., vice chairman of the American Heart Association's Nutrition Committee.

Research has shown that even a modest reduction in weight—5 percent to 10 percent—also can reduce other cardiovascular risk factors like high blood pressure, diabetes and elevated blood cholesterol.

Dr. Eckel, a professor of medicine and physiology at the University of Colorado Health Sciences Center and an expert on obesity, emphasizes that more research needs to be done to determine the role that obesity plays in heart disease. "Today our understanding of obesity and its impact on coronary heart disease is in its infancy—comparable to our understanding of cholesterol's role in heart disease in the mid-1970s," he says.

There are no simple answers as to why obesity is increasing. "However, one reason for the epidemic is that although Americans are eating a lower percentage of total calories from fat, they are eating more calories overall," says Dr. Eckel.

Other significant factors include increasingly sedentary lifestyles among adults and children, according to Dr. Eckel.

Obesity can be treated through lifestyle strategies like calorie restriction, physical activity, medications and, in some cases, surgery.

"Health care providers and the public need to accept that obesity is a chronic disease, just like high blood pressure or high blood cholesterol," says Dr. Eckel. Stress caused me to eat more than anything in my life. If you are under a great deal of stress you will continue to gain weight unless you put the stress to rest!

Ways of Coping

Acute stress can cause:
Uneasiness and concern
Sadness or a heightened sense of energy
Loss of appetite
Alertness
Suppression of the immune system
Increased metabolism and use of body fats
Infertility

Chronic stress can cause:
Anxiety and panic attacks
Depression or melancholia
Anorexia or overeating
Irritability
Lowered resistance to infections
Diabetes or hypertension

Absence of menstruation (amenorrhea) or loss of sex drive

15 tips to relieve stress
Dr. Cregan of the Mayo Clinic says longer working days, less sleep and information overload are the three main sources of stress.
"You have to ask, 'Is more better? Is faster better?' Answering yes has changed the stress levels in our lives,"

says Dr. Creagan. "The average workweek is 50 hours. People now have 90 minutes less sleep than their grandparents did and the volume of information we receive from the Internet, TV, radio, newspapers, magazines and e-mail is overwhelming. We are overstimulated."

Dr. Creagan recommends the following these 15 tips to relieve stress. "Just realize that the only way to survive our stressful existence is to recognize that we have choices and options in the way we live and respond to stress," he says.

1. **Simplify your life.** Cut out some activities or delegate tasks. Use the extra time to relax through such exercises as controlling your breathing, clearing your mind and relaxing your muscles.

2. **View negative situations as positive and a chance to improve your life.** Use humor to reduce or relieve tension.

3. Exercise. It relieves tension and provides a "time out" from stressful situations.

4. Go to bed earlier. More sleep makes you stronger and more able to handle day-to-day life.

5. Reduce or eliminate caffeine consumption. Caffeine is a stimulant.

6. Get a massage.

7. Keep a stress journal. Track what sets you off and learn to prioritize. Do what is most important first.

8. Enjoy yourself. Read a good book or see an uplifting movie.

9. Take a hot bath.

10. Call a friend and strengthen or establish a support network. Make the most of friends and family.

11. Set aside personal time. Limit time spent with negative people.

12. Hug your family and friends.

13. Do volunteer work or start a hobby.

14. Pray or meditate.

15. Take a vacation. Take a day or longer to rejuvenate yourself. Seeking professional help.

How do you know if you are feeling simple stress or something more?
"Bring it up to your primary care provider or your spouse or partner," says Dr. Creagan. "Ask them what they see, and ask yourself if the stress you feel is worth the consequences."
Professional help is important if you feel depressed or have an anxiety disorder—conditions that often are triggered by stress and that often are overlooked. However, stress-induced conditions are manageable and treatable.

Many times I had tried and failed in eating right, as will you. However, these helpful hints will make the road smoother. Jonny Bowden from ivillage.com gives this advice.

1. **The food pyramid is for everyone.** For many people, six to eleven daily servings of grains, breads and cereals is just too much. It has been known to cause bloat, fat and ill health.

2. **There is a perfect diet that will work for everyone.** Some people do fabulously well on vegetarian diets, and some people crash and burn. One size only fits the people who come in that size.

3. **All low-carb diets are like the Atkins Diet.** There are many ways to get the healthful, weight reducing benefits of eating fewer carbs without going on the Atkins plan.

4. **Stress does not make you fat.** The truth is that the stress hormone cortisol leads to carbohydrate cravings and overeating, as well as to abdominal fat.

5. **Metabolisms are all pretty similar.** Metabolisms have as great a range as cars. Some of us are Jaguars and some of us are SUVs. You need to match the right kind of gas (food) with the right kind of engine (metabolism).

6. **Blood type does not make a difference.** Actually, blood type does play a part in weight loss. People with certain blood types are more likely to be allergic or sensitive to certain foods. Those with type O, for example, are far more likely than other types to be hypersensitive to dairy.

7. **A balanced diet will provide you with everything you need.** It's possible to have reasonable health without supplements, but it's virtually impossible to have optimal health without them.

For a long while I was a vegetarian and now I eat poultry and fish. I would, however, like to share the benefits of being a "healthy vegetarian."

Becoming a vegetarian doesn't automatically mean that you'll lose weight. Big helpings of high-fat protein sources (think cheese and peanut butter) can actually cause vegetarians to *gain* weight.

• Vegetarian protein sources include nuts, seeds, legumes (dried beans and peas such as lentils, black beans and garbanzo beans) and soy products such as tofu or tempeh. Some vegetarians include fish and eggs in their food choices as well.

• If you don't use dairy products, choose soy-based alternates for milk, cheese and yogurt. Make sure these products are fortified with calcium, vitamin D and riboflavin for optimum health.

• Be wary of high-fat foods such as cheeses, butter, salad dressing and fried foods.

• Drink water as your primary between-meal beverage.

• Choose whole grains as much as possible to keep hunger at bay.

• Keep a written record of everything you eat and drink to get a better handle on your total food consumption, and identify where you want to make changes.

- Plan ahead for meals and snacks so you know exactly what you plan to eat. Last minute choices tend to be higher in calories and lower in satisfaction.

- Resist the urge to snack on fried chips, snack crackers and candy. Not only do they add unwanted calories, they don't provide any nutritional bonus either!

- Take a daily multivitamin-mineral supplement to fill in any nutritional gaps.

One of the most important foods is fiber. I used these tips to jump start my intake of fiber.

Your mother probably called it "roughage." Doctors and nutrition experts call it "'fiber"—the part of plant-based foods that is not absorbed by the body. And they say most of you should eat more of it.

You need between 20 grams and 35 grams of fiber each day. To make sure you get the fiber you need:

START your day with a high-fiber breakfast cereal (5 or more grams of fiber per serving). Opt for cereals with the word "bran" or "fiber" in the name. Or add a few table-spoons of unprocessed wheat bran to your favorite cereal.

SWITCH to whole-grain breads. These list "whole wheat," "whole-wheat flour" or another whole grain as the first ingredient on the label.

EAT more whole grains and whole-grain products. Experiment with brown rice, barley and whole-wheat pasta.

TAKE advantage of today's ready-to-use vegetables. Mix frozen broccoli into prepared spaghetti sauce. Snack on baby carrots.

EAT more beans, peas and lentils. Add kidney beans to canned soup or a green salad. Or make nachos with black bean dip, baked tortilla chips and salsa.

MAKE snacks count. Fresh and dried fruit, raw vegetables, popcorn and whole-grain crackers are all good sources of fiber.

EAT fruit at every meal. Apples, bananas, oranges, pears and berries are especially good sources of fiber.

SUBSTITUTE whole-grain flour for white flour when baking bread. Whole-grain flour is heavier than white flour. In yeast breads, use a bit more yeast or let the dough rise longer. When using baking powder, increase it by 1 teaspoon for every 3 cups of whole-grain flour.

To avoid bloating and gas problems, increase your fiber intake gradually. And drink plenty of water as you increase your fiber to promote regularity.

My favorite way of eating is like the people in the Mediterranean because I love fruits, vegetables and grains.

Picture the sunny Mediterranean. You probably imagine warm days, blue skies and the glistening sea. But don't leave out the food.

In fact, if you're interested in a long and healthy life, you probably should try to eat more like the people in

Crete, Greece, or southern Italy. Research indicates that the Mediterranean eating style may help prevent heart attacks as well as reduce the risk of some cancers.

Gathering evidence

The value of eating Mediterranean style came into focus in the 1950s and 1960s. The lifestyle and dietary habits of more than 12,000 men were studied in seven countries, including the United States.

The study showed that men living in Crete and other parts of Greece were least likely to develop heart disease. For Greek men the premature death rate from heart attack was 90 percent lower than that of American men. And Greek men enjoyed the longest life expectancy in the world.

More recent studies have shown that people who have had a heart attack and then followed a Mediterranean eating style reduced their risk of a second heart attack by as much as 70 percent.

What made the difference? Food appeared to play a big role.

Plates in the Mediterranean traditionally are loaded with fresh fruits and vegetables, grains of all types and legumes such as beans, lentils and peas. People eat very little red meat and consume fatty dairy products infrequently.

Mediterranean dishes are also enhanced with olive oil, a monounsaturated fat. Olive oil is generally used in place of saturated fats found in products made from fatty meats and dairy foods, such as shortenings, butter and creamy spreads, and in place of polyunsaturated fats found in other vegetable oils.

Here's to your health

Olive oil appears to help lower blood levels of low-density lipoprotein (LDL) cholesterol, which add to the risk of heart disease, without lowering the levels of high-density lipoprotein (HDL) cholesterol, which protects against heart disease. The benefits of eating Mediterranean likely extend beyond protection from heart disease, though. The other components of Mediterranean fare—whole grains, legumes and plenty of fresh fruits and vegetables—are packed with other substances that seem to enhance health.

For instance, the dietary fiber found in whole grains, fruits and vegetables may offer some protection against colon problems. Fruits and vegetables also give your body a regular source of phytochemicals and antioxidants. These substances are thought to neutralize free radicals—harmful substances in your body that may contribute to cancer and heart disease.

Red wine with meals is also a Mediterranean tradition. In moderation, the wine appears to play a role in increasing HDL cholesterol levels.

Time for a change?

Nutrition experts have been encouraging Americans to shift their diet to more plant-based foods, aiming daily for 6 to 11 servings of grains and 5 to 9 servings of fruits and vegetables. Typically, most Americans fall far short of this.

To move toward a plant-based, Mediterranean eating style, try to:

- **Go meatless several times a week.** Look for recipes that make vegetables, pasta, nuts and legumes the main event.

- **Explore a variety of grains.** Try recipes that feature grains and grain products such as barley, bulgur (cracked wheat), brown rice or couscous. Enjoy whole grain breads and pastas too.

- **Expand your flavoring techniques.** Use fresh herbs, garlic, grated lemon or capers.

- **Serve fruit at every meal.** Make fruit more than just a dessert.

Use cheese as a flavoring or seasoning. Use small amounts of cheese to enhance other foods. Crumble feta cheese on hearty bean soup or sprinkle some fresh Parmesan on sauteed vegetables.

I had to work very hard at losing weight, but I had to work harder at being smarter to really lose the weight. I followed these guidelines:

"Build both strength and stamina."

<u>Proper form</u>

Form is everything when it comes to resistance training. Ideally, people should work with a fitness professional to learn how to do the exercises properly. There also are good books available to help you get started.

Avoid jerky movements. Concentrate on moving the weight slowly through the full range of motion. Use a mirror to monitor your movements. As you do the exercise, remember to breathe. Don't hold your breath as you try to do a repetition, just breathe normally throughout the motion.

Also, don't forget to rest. If you follow the program as designed, you will likely see noticeable changes that may tempt you to overtrain. If you don't get proper rest, you risk injury and an interruption of your weight training program. When you are tired, rest. Don't try to push too far, too fast.

The training groups listed below are arranged in an order that allows your body to warm up with abdominal and chest exercises. Be sure to stretch after your training sessions to help maintain flexibility, another aspect of overall fitness. Add some aerobic exercise at least 3 days a week and you'll be well on your way to becoming fit.

Stretching:

A key to avoiding athletic injuries

"No pain, no gain" has been a credo of some coaches and athletes regarding warm-up stretches. Here are better words to keep in mind while you stretch: "No pain, no pain."

"You can do a disservice to yourself when you stretch past the point of pain," says Edward Laskowski, M.D., co-director of the Mayo Clinic Sports Medicine Center, Rochester, Minn. "You should never hold a painful stretch. You should back off just to where it's not painful, and that's what you want to hold during the duration of the stretch."

The goal of routine stretching exercises is to maximize your joints' range of motion. Flexibility, cardiovascular conditioning and resistance training are the three broad objectives to focus on as you maintain your body for the rigors and enjoyment of sports. Proper stretching actually lengthens the muscle tissue, making it less tight and, therefore, less prone to trauma and tears. A stretching routine also feels good and can be a relaxing period of your day.

<u>Don't stretch these rules</u>

Dr. Laskowski advises the following to get the most out of your stretching program.

- **Everybody's different.** We all aren't gymnasts. Focus on maintaining adequate flexibility for your own sports and activity level.

- **Be sport-specific.** Different sports emphasize different muscle groups. Concentrate on the range of motions and the muscle groups that you're likely to use in your sport.

- **Start slowly.** For example: A ballet dancer begins slowly, with one hand on the bar, before beginning high kicks out on the floor.

- **Hold your stretch.** It takes time to lengthen tissue safely. Hold your stretches at least 30 seconds—and up to a minute with a particularly tight muscle or problem area.

- **Stretch heated muscles.** Stretching a cold muscle can strain and irritate the tissue. Warm up first. For instance, walk before you jog and jog before you run. It's most beneficial to stretch *after* you exercise, when the muscle is heated by blood flow and is more accommodating to stretching.

- **Do not bounce.** Bouncing can cause microtrauma in the muscle, which heals itself with scar tissue. The scar tissue tightens the muscle even more, making you less flexible—and more prone to pain.

- **Think equality.** Strive for balance in flexibility on each side of your body. For example, if one hamstring is tighter than the other, you may be more prone to injury.

- **Don't be afraid to ask.** A sports medicine specialist, athletic trainer, physical therapist or health-club advisor may help improve your stretching technique.

New research

Mayo sports medicine doctors are researching whether relaxation of a muscle may be an important part of achieving flexibility, perhaps apart from or in combination with stretching. Anecdotally, they've observed a high degree of flexibility in tight-muscled people while they are under general anesthesia—even though their muscles are structurally the same as when they are awake. Although it's too early to draw conclusions, the theory behind this new research is that stimulation from your central nervous system influences your muscles' flexibility and that relaxing your muscles may be a viable method of enhancing your joints' range of motion.

Resolving to exercise? Jump-start your program

Regular exercise is easy to lay aside because, frankly, it may seem like the least important thing on your schedule. But exercise is important. Studies show that regular exercise can give you more energy, a better quality of life, a healthier body composition, better balance and coordination, improved sleep and longer life expectancy.

As you age, you have much to gain from getting and staying fit. Exercising regularly and staying physically active can prevent or delay serious problems like coronary artery disease, stroke, type 2 diabetes, cancer, bone loss and osteoporosis. In some cases it even may improve your health if you already have a disease or disability.

The good news is you can increase your fitness level with as little as 30 minutes of low to moderately intense physical activity a day, as recommended by the Centers for Disease Control and Prevention and the American College of Sports Medicine. The most important thing is to incorporate physical activity into your lifestyle and maintain it, according to Edward Laskowski, M.D., co-director of the Sports Medicine Center at Mayo Clinic, Rochester, Minn.

"Consistency is more important than intensity," Dr. Laskowski says. "And you can accumulate short periods of exercise throughout the day rather than doing it all at once. Studies show that three 10-minute doses of exercise can be just as effective for heart health as one 30-minute session."

So throw out the idea that you have to spend your life at the gym to be fit. Adopt a new mind-set and think of exercise as an ongoing part of your day. The best time to begin exercising is now. It's never too late to start, even if you've never exercised before.

Building blocks of fitness

Three basic types of activities can improve your health and make you more fit:

- **Aerobic or endurance exercises** increase your breathing and heart rate to improve the health of your heart, lungs and circulatory system. These exercises involve repeated contraction of large muscle groups but don't require excessive speed. The net result of aerobic exercise is increased stamina and endurance.

- **Strength and balance exercises** build stronger muscles to improve posture, balance and coordination. Strength training also increases your metabolism, increases lean muscle mass, supports joints, slows bone loss, cuts the risk of injury and makes you feel more energetic.

- **Stretching exercises** increase the range in which you can bend and stretch joints, muscles and ligaments. Flexibility helps prevent joint and muscle pain and injury.

Making fitness a part of your life

So how do you begin incorporating these activities into your life? First of all, it may be a good idea to consult your physician before you begin an exercise program. If you are over 40 and sedentary, a smoker, overweight or have a chronic health condition, such as heart disease, high blood pressure, osteoporosis, kidney disease, liver disease or arthritis, it's essential that you see your physician first. He or she can help you develop an exercise program that is best for you.

After determining your appropriate level of exercise, commit yourself to being active. This doesn't mean you won't have setbacks or take breaks. The key is to keep on going even after an occasional layoff.

A typical activity session might include a 5-minute warm-up, 30 minutes of aerobic activity, which you can build up to, 10 to 20 minutes of strength and balance exercises, and 5 to 10 minutes of cooling down and stretching. However, you can spread activities throughout the day.

Activity tips

To help you get started, Dr. Laskowski gives the following advice for each type of activity:

Aerobic and Endurance. Find something you enjoy doing. Boredom is the primary reason exercise programs fail. "The ideal piece of equipment," says Dr. Laskowski, "is something you like to do."

Aerobic activity doesn't have to be expensive or inconvenient. Grab your neighbor and take a brisk walk around the block. Watch television while walking on a treadmill. Go hiking or play hopscotch with your children. Take a night off and go dancing. Wash your car. Walk up the stairs instead of taking the elevator. Park in the far corner of the parking lot. Short doses of exercise add up. Varying your activities will also make it easier to keep them up.

Remember to start out slowly. Don't go for dramatic increases. Instead, build up gradually by adding a minute a week to your aerobic activity. Mark your progress on your own personal activity log. "One of the best ways to change a habit is to keep track of it," says Dr. Laskowski. "An exercise log will give you a visual record of improvement and motivate you to keep going."

During aerobic exercise you should be able to carry on a conversation with a companion. If you are too winded to talk, you're probably pushing too hard.

If you have arthritis or joint pain, do low-or nonimpact activities, such as riding a stationary or recumbent bike, or do pool exercises. Even if you don't like to swim, walking in the shallow end can provide aerobic benefits, and the buoyancy of the water will take stress off your joints.

Also, try before you buy. Exercise equipment too often ends up in the classified ads rather than in use.

Strength and Balance. Each decade between the ages of 30 and 70 you lose about 5 percent of your lean muscle mass. Strength training can slow this aging process.

Free weights are a great way to build lean muscle mass because they simulate what you do in real life, like carrying boxes or lifting a tired child. You usually can buy weights by the pound. A used sporting goods store might be a good place to look. When you first begin a program, try higher repetitions of a lower weight. As you improve, aim to lift the amount of weight that exhausts your muscles after 12 repetitions. If doing 12 repetitions is too easy, try adding more weight. If you can't complete 12 repetitions, use less weight.

Again, start out slowly. Studies show that doing one set of 12 repetitions is just as effective as doing three sets.

Make an appointment with a certified professional to learn proper technique. Improper technique is one of the leading causes of injuries.

Remember to work all the major muscle groups: abdominals, legs, chest, back, shoulders and arms. Balance your workout. Strengthen muscles on opposite sides of a joint equally. For example, work your triceps, biceps, hamstrings (the back of your thigh) and quadriceps (the front of your thigh) as well as the muscles on the back of your shoulder (posterior deltoid) and the muscles on the front of your shoulder (anterior deltoids and pectorals). It's best to perform strength training two or three days a week.

Flexibility and Stretching. This aspect of fitness can be especially frustrating. Your vision of flexibility might be akin to what you would expect from a ballerina or a tae kwon do artist, but your body is telling you otherwise. It's important to remember that everyone's genetic set point for flexibility is different. Your ability to stretch might vary greatly from your best friend's. However, this is an area in which you can improve and gain more range of motion.

Although it's good to stretch before and after exercise, you might not have time to do both. The ideal time to stretch is when your muscles are heated up—after you've exercised. Dr. Laskowski recommends beginning your exercise with a slow version of your preferred activity that day. If you are walking, start out slowly and gradually build up speed. Then stretch when you have finished your walk.

When stretching, hold your stretches for at least 30 seconds. Focus on those muscles you use the most. If you play golf or do racquet sports, focus on your shoulder muscles. If you walk or run, stretch calf muscles, hamstrings and quadriceps. Also remember to keep your back flexible. Your back muscles support your spine, and a healthy spine is crucial to any activity.

To a better life

It's easy to get sidetracked and neglect regular exercise. Remember, however, that it takes only about 30 minutes a day to create a significant change in your quality of life. Make a list of all the benefits that come with regular exercise and put it in a highly visible place. Encourage your friends and family to be active as well. Taking care of your body is one of the most valuable gifts you can give yourself.

You just have to keep at it, build on your successes and not be derailed when you run into obstacles.

Water

Water, Water, Water is what you must drink every single day that you live. I drink about 3 to 4 quarts a day depending on my workout routine.

The experts at Mayo Clinic agree:

You've heard it a thousand times: Drink eight glasses of water a day. Even though this is just an estimated amount for most people, you don't do it. You're drowning in excuses—you don't like the taste, it's not convenient, you never remember. No big deal, you think—it's not affecting your health.

You're all wet. Getting enough water is crucial to your health. You couldn't survive without it. Yet, surveys indicate that many Americans don't drink enough.

To understand why water is so important, you have to know what it does for your body. So grab a tall glassful and read on.

Waterlogged

Your body is one-half to four-fifths water, depending on how much body fat you have. Water makes up nearly 85 percent or your brain, about 80 percent of your blood and about 70 percent of your lean muscle. (Because there are a lot of tissues that have less water, the average is about 50 percent.)

Every system in your body depends on water. Its roles are impressive. Water:

- regulates your body temperature

- removes wastes

- carries nutrients and oxygen to your cells

- cushions your joints

- helps prevent constipation

- lessens the burden on your kidneys and liver by removing some of the toxins

- helps dissolve vitamins, minerals and other nutrients to make them accessible to your body

Lack of water can lead to dehydration. Even slight dehydration can sap your energy and make you feel lethargic. Dehydration poses a particular health risk for the very young and very old.

Prevention floats

Besides helping your body run smoothly, there's some evidence that water helps prevent certain diseases. People who have had kidney stones can prevent further stones from forming by drinking lots of fluid. And in one study, women who drank more than five glasses of water a day had a risk of colon cancer that was 45 percent less than others in the study who drank two or fewer glasses a day.

Why water?

You lose about 10 cups of fluid a day through sweating, exhaling, urinating and bowel movements. Drinking water isn't the only way to replace those fluids. You also get water from other beverages and even from foods.

In an average diet, it's estimated that solid foods provide between three and four cups of water a day. But because it's difficult to estimate the amount of water solid foods contribute, it's recommended that you only count fluids toward meeting your goal of eight glasses a day. But that's only a ballpark estimate. To better determine how much water you specifically need each day, divide your weight in half. Your answer is the approximate number of fluid ounces you should drink daily.

Eight glasses is the average. Some people need more, while others can get by on less. Exercising or engaging in any activity that causes you to perspire and dehydrate increases your water requirement, as do hot, humid or cold weather and high altitudes. Keep in mind that sports drinks are better than water if you're exerting yourself for

90 minutes or more at a time; 60 minutes if the activity is particularly intense or temperatures are very hot.

Some beverages, such as those with caffeine and alcohol, are dehydrating, so if you drink them, you need even more water to compensate.

Water safety

Three out of four Americans are concerned about the safety of their tap water, which has led to a dramatic increase in sales of water filtration systems and bottled water. Is your water safe to drink? Most people's tap water is fine. It's regulated by the Environmental Protection Agency (EPA) for safety and purity and chlorinated to destroy most organisms that can spread disease. However, small amounts of microbiological and chemical contaminants are allowed within EPA limits of safety or when water treatment equipment breaks down.

The EPA requires public suppliers to notify you if your water doesn't meet safety standards. In 1993, for instance, health officials warned residents in some areas of Milwaukee of a parasite known as cryptosporidium. Resistant to chlorine and filtration, it can cause severe health problems for people with impaired immune systems and can cause nausea and diarrhea in healthy people. Although cryptosporidium outbreaks are rare, Milwaukee's proved to be the largest outbreak of a waterborne disease in the United States, affecting more than 400,000 people.

H20 4 U

If you're healthy and not in any dehydrating conditions, some experts say you can use your thirst as an indicator of when to drink. Others believe that if you're thirsty, you've already started to dehydrate. Play it safe by making a conscious effort to keep yourself hydrated. Drink a glass of water when you get up and another when you go to bed. Keep a bottle with you during the day or take regular water breaks. Drink water with meals and avoid relying on soda to provide your fluid needs. Getting enough water just might buoy your health.

What's your thirst telling you?

As is often the case with your health, it's best to start with the obvious: Your thirst tells you to drink. For healthy people under normal circumstances, thirst is a reliable mechanism to indicate the body's need for more fluid.

"However, your thirst doesn't tell you exactly what to drink. It just tells you that you're thirsty," says Kenneth G. Berge, M.D., associate medical editor of Mayo Health Oasis. "Of course, billions of dollars are made by persuading you to reflexively reach for a soft drink or something like that, when really the best choice usually is water."

How much to drink?

You may have read or heard that you need at least eight glasses of water per day. This quantity won't hurt a healthy adult. But Dr. Berge says such one-size-fits-all answer fails to tell the whole story about the body's necessary balance of fluid intake and loss. What is lost must be replaced to maintain a fluid balance. Dehydration poses a particular health risk for the very young and the very old.

Not all fluid replacement must come from water. Other drinks consist mostly of water. Foods contain water as well. However, as mentioned earlier, your thirst is generally a good guide for when you need to replace fluids and water is generally the best choice. "If you are normal and have a normal set of kidneys and lungs, I think the maximum amount of water tolerated is huge and the minimum is less than eight glasses a day," Dr. Berge says.

Caffeinated and alcoholic beverages are actually dehydrating because they increase urine output, so don't count on those to replenish fluid loss.

Are their exceptions?

Of course! For example, if you have kidney stones, drinking eight or more glasses of water a day is highly recommended. You also should drink extra amounts of water when you are experiencing any dehydrating conditions (e.g., hot, humid or cold weather, high altitudes, physical exertion, etc.).

What does the body do with all that water?

Among other things, water regulates the body's temperature through perspiration, carries away wastes in the urine and moves nutrients and other substances throughout the body. There's tremendous movement of water to and from organs and tissues in your body. Blood itself is more than 80 percent water. A healthy person's urine output is a very small fraction of the total quantity of fluid filtered by the kidneys. Most is reabsorbed and used elsewhere in the body.

What can excessive thirst mean?

Increased thirst and increased urination (both in volume and frequency) can be symptoms of diabetes mellitus. Excessive thirst and urination also are symptoms of diabetes insipidus. Diabetes mellitus is due to a deficiency of or resistance to insulin, a hormone produced by the pancreas that enables your body to use glucose to provide cells with energy. This is not to be confused with diabetes insipidus, which results from a deficiency of antidiuretic hormone (ADH). A shortage of ADH, which is produced by the posterior lobe of the pituitary gland in the brain, causes your body to lose control of its water balance. If you notice unexplained increases in thirst and urination, consult your physician to determine the cause. There are other possible causes to be considered. Some people consume excessive amounts of water and experience increased urine output not associated with any underlying disease.

What about hydration during physical exertion?

Thirst is not always an adequate indicator of your body's need for fluid replenishment during exercise. Studies show that during vigorous exercise, an important amount of your fluid reserves may be lost before you are aware of thirst. Make sure you are sufficiently hydrated before, during and after exercise. Again, water is your best bet. Sports drinks are generally not necessary unless you are exerting yourself for 90 minutes or more (60 minutes if the activity is particularly intense or temperatures are very hot). During exercise, it's recommended to replenish fluids at least every 20 minutes. Remember, your body has limits to its ability to adjust to fluid loss.

Sleep Like a Baby!

While beginning my life change, I began to note that if I did not get 8 to 10 hours of sleep a night my workouts would be sluggish and simply painful. I would not have enthusiasm for the workout and I would begin to feel melancholy. When I would sleep 8 or more hours a night, I could move mountains and even climb a few. This is why I consider "sleeping" part of protecting the beautiful self. Also, I noted that when I did get enough sleep and rest, I began to lose weight faster and at a steadier pace. Here are a few tips that I found useful to sleep better.

10 tips for better sleep

More than 100 million people in the United States don't get a good night's sleep on a regular basis. And an additional 33 million Americans have occasional sleepless nights. Sleeping well is not a luxury, it is a necessity.

Sleep deprivation impairs memory, reaction time and alertness. Tired people are less productive at work, less patient with others and less interactive in relationships. Sleep deprivation can also be dangerous.

A study by the American Sleep Apnea Association and Stanford University's Sleep Disorders Clinic and Research

Center found that inadequate sleep causes problems similar to drinking too much alcohol. When a tired driver takes the wheel, the results can be disastrous. The National Highway Traffic Safety Administration reports that sleepy drivers cause at least 100,000 crashes each year—40,000 result in injuries and 1,550 are fatal.

<u>10 tips for better sleep</u>

"Adults need 8 full hours of sleep and teens need 9 hours and 15 minutes," says John W. Shepard Jr., M.D., medical director of the Mayo Clinic Sleep Disorders Center, Rochester, Minn. "However, the average person only gets 7 hours and 25 minutes of sleep a night."

The following tips from Dr. Shepard can help you achieve restful sleep. You don't have to use every tip on the list. "What works for one person doesn't always work for another," says Dr. Shepard.

Try one or two or a combination until you have enough quality sleep to feel alert and well rested.

1. Stick to a schedule and don't sleep late on weekends. If you sleep late on Saturday and Sunday morning, you'll get Sunday night insomnia. Instead, go to bed and get up at about the same time every day. "You don't need to rely on an alarm clock to wake up when you get enough sleep," says Dr. Shepard.

2. Don't eat or drink a lot before bedtime. Eat a light dinner about 2 hours before sleeping. If you drink too much liquid before sleeping, you'll wake up repeatedly in the night for trips to the bathroom.

• Don't eat spicy or fatty foods. They cause heartburn.

- Don't have a midnight snack. If you get the munchies, eat something that triggers serotonin, which makes you sleepy. Carbohydrates (bread or cereal) or foods containing the amino acid L-tryptophan (milk, tuna, or turkey) will do the trick.
- Don't drink alcohol near bedtime. It may cause you to wake up repeatedly, snore and possibly develop sleep apnea.

3. Avoid caffeine and nicotine. They are addictive stimulants and keep you awake. Smokers experience withdrawal symptoms at night, and they have a harder time both falling asleep and waking up.

4. Exercise. If you're trying to sleep better, the best time to exercise is in the afternoon. Physical activity enhances the deep, refreshing stage of sleep.

5. A slightly cool room is ideal for sleeping. This mimics your internal temperature drop during sleep, so turn off the heat and save on fuel bills.

- If you tend to get cold, use blankets. Try sleeping in warmer nightclothes and wear socks. Studies show that warm hands and feet induce sleep quickly.
- If you overheat at night, wear light nightclothes and sleep under a single sheet. Use an air conditioner or fan to keep the room cool.
- Use a dehumidifier if you are bothered by moist air. Use a humidifier if you are bothered by dry air. Signs of dry air irritation include a sore throat, nosebleeds or a dry throat.

6. Sleep only at night. Daytime naps steal hours from nighttime slumber. Limit daytime sleep to 20-minute, power naps.

- If you work nights, keep window coverings closed so that sunlight, which interferes with the body's internal clock, doesn't interrupt your sleep.
- If you have a day job and sleep at night, but still have trouble waking, leave the window covering open and let the sun's light wake you up.

7. Keep it quiet. Silence is more conducive to sleep. Turn off the radio and TV. Use earplugs, a fan or some other source of constant, soothing, background noise to mask sound that you cannot control, such as a busy street, trains, airplanes or even a snoring partner. Double-pane windows and heavy curtains also muffle outside noise.

8. Make your bed. "A good bed is subjective and different for each person. Make sure you have a bed that is comfortable and offers orthopedic, correct sleep," says Dr. Shepard.

- If you share your bed, make sure there is enough room for two.
- Use your bed only for sleep and sex.
- Go to bed when you are tired and turn out the lights. If you don't fall asleep in 15 minutes, get up and do something else. Go back to bed when you are tired.
- Do not agonize about falling asleep. The stress will only prevent sleep.

9. Soak and sack out. Taking a hot shower or bath before bed helps bring on sleep because they can relax the tense muscles.

10.Don't rely on sleeping pills. Check with your doctor before using sleeping pills. Make sure the pills won't interact with other medications or with an existing medical condition.

- Use the lowest dosage and never mix alcohol and sleeping pills.
- If you feel sleepy or dizzy during the day, talk to your doctor about changing the dosage or discontinuing the pills.

Now lets get down to the nuts and bolts of it all. What do you really need to do to get yourself into the weight loss mode? Dr. Clark of the Mayo Clinic gives the best advice:

<u>Preparing yourself for weight loss</u>

Matthew M. Clark, Ph.D., is a clinical psychologist who helps people with the behavioral and attitudinal aspects of weight loss and weight maintenance. If you and your doctor have determined that weight loss is a necessary health goal for you, you may find some of Dr. Clark's strategies useful to help enhance and maintain your motivation for losing weight.

Is it important to psych yourself up before starting a weight-loss program?

Clark: According to surveys, most people stop a diet after the first week or two. Anticipating barriers may help reduce this problem. When people start a weight-loss program, it's my experience that they frequently don't think through the long-term work and lifestyle changes that are involved. This lack of planning leads to dropout. You need to consider several things ahead of time: "How's my motivation? How's my stress level? How's my life in general going?"

What are the biggest attitudinal obstacles people face?
Clark: I'd split it into two main areas. One is lifestyle issues. To lose weight, you have to incorporate exercise into your life and change the way you're eating. That requires time and effort. You have to find time to exercise 30 minutes a day and plan and prepare meals. You have to ask yourself: "Am I so busy taking care of work and family that it's going to be too difficult for me to commit long-term to that kind of effort?" The other area is psychological. Some people need to address psychological issues, such as clinical depression or an eating disorder, before they can lose weight. You need to treat these problems first in order to be successful at long-term weight loss. Additionally, people and practitioners should look at whether there are perceived positive aspects to being overweight. For example, perhaps the extra weight offers protection from unwanted sexual attention in personal or professional relationships. If that's the case, addressing this issue might be necessary for success.

How can you tell which people are dealing with lifestyle issues and which are dealing with psychological issues?
Clark: For those who've had difficulty maintaining their weight loss, I ask them what made it difficult for them to maintain their weight loss. They might give lifestyle answers, such as they started working more and stopped going to the health club. Or they might say they thought if they lost weight their relationships would improve. That's an indication of psychological issues.

OK, so what can you do to psych yourself up?

Clark: There's an approach called decisional balance that's been used more for quitting smoking or problem drinking, but also applies to weight management. You think about all the good things about losing weight, such as having more energy and improving your health. Then you look at the negatives, such as finding the time to exercise or getting the family to agree to dietary changes. You can increase motivation by focusing on the pros and coming up with solutions to the cons. If one downside is that you don't know how to find time for exercise, perhaps your employer has a gym you can use on your lunch hour. Then remind yourself how your health will improve if you lose weight. By thinking of these things, you may be able to increase your motivation. Another technique has to do with building your self-confidence. Frequently people have failed at previous weight-loss attempts, so their confidence and motivation for starting a new program are low. You need to focus on what has worked for you in the past. Maybe you benefited from the group support in one program. Or you found walking with a friend more enjoyable than going to aerobics classes. You need to incorporate these proven elements into your new effort. Look at your previous successes and build on them. Also, it's important to set reasonable goals. Some people expect to lose a lot of weight each week or too much weight overall. They get disappointed, motivation decreases, and they drop out. For most people, losing 1/2 to 1 pound a week is reasonable. It's most beneficial long-term to make slow, steady changes. You also need to make sure that the way you go about losing weight is appropriate for both the amount of weight you want to lose and for your health status. If someone wants to lose 20 pounds, I wouldn't recommend the same program as I would for someone who needs to lose 100 pounds. Nor would the program be the same for someone who's healthy as it would be for someone who has health problems. Talk to your doctor about how much weight is healthy and realistic for you to lose and what's the best approach for you. Your doctor may refer you to a dietitian or an endocrinologist who specializes in obesity.

What would you do if you needed to lose weight?

Clark: I'd first get advice and an OK from a doctor. Then I'd meet with a dietitian to choose a flexible meal plan. I'd also consult with an exercise specialist to develop a personalized exercise program. I'd ask myself, do I need to join a health club or can I walk around the neighborhood with a friend? Where can I get either weight-management support (such as from a diet buddy whom I can talk to about meal plans and exercise) or emotional support (such as from a significant other) for making major lifestyle changes? I'd also anticipate having a relapse and plan for how I'd recover from an overeating episode. Anticipate relapses and know that you're not going to be perfect.

What do you think about using an over-the-counter (OTC) diet aid as a jump start for the first 2 weeks?

Clark: I haven't seen any published research that shows any benefits of the OTC products. As an alternative, how about a lifestyle jump start? What if you took extra time to plan meals for 2 weeks and grocery shopped ahead of time? Or you could enlist someone to exercise with you 3 to 5 days a week for the first 2 weeks. That would be a healthy lifestyle jump start.

How important is keeping a food diary?

Clark: In clinical programs, having people write down what they eat is the best predictor of weight loss. Research shows a strong relationship between keeping food records and meeting weekly weight-loss and behavioral goals. However, some people not involved in structured programs can be successful by avoiding certain high-fat foods, eating regular meals and limiting portions.

How important is group support?

Clark: For people who aren't getting support elsewhere, it's very important. A lot of people don't receive support for weight loss. Support can be emotional or active problem solving. Both are important to a successful program.

What's willpower, and is it a valid concept?

Clark: Psychologists are trying to focus on self-control rather than willpower. Self-control is, "Ice cream is my problem food, I'm not going to keep it in the house." Willpower is, "I'm going to keep buying it, but I won't eat it. I'll prove to myself how strong my willpower is." Self-control is planning for success ahead of time.

Are there psychological characteristics common to people who succeed at losing weight?

Clark: Researchers haven't been able to identify what psychologically enables someone to be successful long-term. That's a question I'm trying to look at. I assume people are more successful if they focus on the pros of weight management and build their self-confidence. Set reasonable expectations and have a willingness to address psychological issues if necessary.

Is it harder to get and stay motivated when you have a lot of weight to lose?

Clark: The common theory is the more weight you have to lose, the more difficult it is to be motivated. But most people will tell you it's difficult no matter how much weight they need to lose. You just have to keep at it, build on your successes and not be derailed when you run into obstacles.

When you begin to change your life, get excited about what's to come. Smile to yourself. Change doesn't have to be a bad thing. Pretend like you are waiting for a $50, 000 check in the mail. GET EXCITED! If you expect all the wonderful things that you deserve, they will come. Take it one principle at a time and be patient with yourself. Keep your plans and dreams up front and to yourself, and only share them with those who will be supportive. Ask God for what you don't have if your faith is too small, put your dreams in God's hands. If you don't know how to forgive, ask God to help you. If you don't know where to begin, sit still and pray on that too. There is incredible power in prayer. There is no dream too big or impossible. The first step in changing your life is admitting to yourself that how you are living today is not the way you want to live the rest of your life. You deserve joy and sweet peace. Begin today. Love yourself enough to try hard. Believe that anything is possible through God. If you dare to become your own Superhero, rest assured that life will never be the same!

ACKNOWLEDGEMENTS

I have come a long way and I have a long, long way to go on this spiritual journey of life. There are so many people who have helped me in my pursuit of wellness that it is inevitable that I will unintentionally forget someone. Please forgive me. I must first thank God for all I am and all that I will ever be! Big hugs and lots of love to my mother Betty Heath and my father Harrison for bringing me to life and especially you mommy who taught me the secrets of becoming my own Superhero! I thank my 7 brothers and sisters and my many nieces and nephews who have loved and supported me on the journey. I give many thanks to Francis Saamoa Acquaye for your sincere friendship and the incredible amount of help and support you have given me. My sincerest thanks to Suzette Williams for being and staying my best friend for over 30 years! To my little princess Lora Doumbia I thank you for letting me love and mother you. Thank you Dr. Gale Blakely for saving my life. I anticipate the day I can show you my gratitude. Ms. Lissette Norman for loaning me your incredible editing skills and being patient and loving with the manuscript and me! My gratitude to Dr. Maya Angelou (the Queen) for believing in me and inspiring the new front cover. To everyone at iUniverse who has helped make my book a success I thank you so much!

Lissette Norman is a prose and poetry writer from Harlem, NY. She now lives in Staten Island. Her work has been published in an anthology, Moving Beyond Boundaries (1995) as well as in a college textbook, A Dialogic Approach (1995). Her poetry was published in Mosaic Literary Magazine (Summer 2000 issue). Her articles have also appeared in several publications. She received her BA in English (1992) from Binghamton University. Lisse2000365@cs.com

Michelle L. Heath is a motivational speaker, writer, poet, actress and has been a professional nurse for over 20 years. Michelle has spoken for the State Department of Education, and in colleges and universities. Michelle currently lives in New York. You can reach Michelle L. Heath at www.superhero7.com

BIBLIOGRAPHY

Depak Chopra, The Seven Spiritual Laws of Success, Amber Allen Publishing 1994

Jonny Bowden, Weight loss Coach and Nutrition Expert of ivillage.com

John W. Shepard Jr., M.D. medical director of the Mayo Clinic for Sleep Disorders Rochester, Minn.

Kenneth G. Berge, M. D. associate medical editor of Mayo Health Oasis

Edward laskowski M. D., co–director of the Mayo Clinic Sports Medicine Center Rochester, Minn

Matthew M. Clark PH.D of Mayo Clinic Rochester, Minn

0-595-15082-9

Printed in the United States
968400004B

9 780595 150823